D1591526

Supporting Children with Down's Syndrome

THE FARMINGTON COMMUNITY LIBRARY
FARMINGTON HILLS BRANCH
32737 WEST TWELVE MILE ROAD
FARMINGTON HILLS, MI 48334-3302
(248) 553-0300

This practical resource contains a wealth of valuable advice and tried-and-tested strategies for supporting children and young people with Down's syndrome. Fully updated with the 2014 SEND Code of Practice, this text describes the different types of difficulties experienced by pupils with Down's syndrome and helps practitioners to understand their diverse needs.

The wide-ranging chapters explore a variety of topics, including:

- Defining the profile of a pupil with Down's syndrome
- Guidelines for working with pupils
- Addressing behaviour issues
- The use of ICT
- Home/school liaison
- Assessment

It provides guidance and practical strategies for SENCOs, teachers and other professionals and parents, helping them to feel more confident, and be more effective in supporting learners in a variety of settings. It also provides materials for in-house training sessions and features useful checklists, templates and photocopiable resources.

Lisa Bentley – Educational Consultant, Downright Special Education, UK

Ruth Dance – Educational Psychologist, Hull Learning Services, UK

Elizabeth Morling – Series Editor, SEN Consultant and former Head of the Education Service for Physical Disability, Hull City Council, UK

Susan Miller – Senior Psychologist, City Educational Psychological Service, Hull City Council, UK

Susan Wong – Parent Representative, Hull and District Down's Syndrome Association, UK

DEC 1 4 2017

Helping Everyone Achieve ■■■

nasen is a professional membership association that supports all those who work with or care for children and young people with special and additional educational needs. Members include teachers, teaching assistants, support workers, other educationalists, students and parents.

nasen supports its members through policy documents, journals, its magazine Special!, publications, professional development courses, regional networks and newsletters. Its website contains more current information such as responses to government consultations. **nasen's** published documents are held in very high regard both in the UK and internationally.

Other titles published in association with the National Association for Special Educational Needs (nasen):

Language for Learning in the Secondary School: A practical guide for supporting students with speech, language and communication needs
Sue Hayden and Emma Jordan
2012/pb: 978-0-415-61975-2

Using Playful Practice to Communicate with Special Children
Margaret Corke
2012/pb: 978-0-415-68767-6

The Equality Act for Educational Professionals: A simple guide to disability and inclusion in schools
Geraldine Hills
2012/pb: 978-0-415-68768-3

More Trouble with Maths: A teacher's complete guide to identifying and diagnosing mathematical difficulties
Steve Chinn
2012/pb: 978-0-415-67013-5

Dyslexia and Inclusion: Classroom approaches for assessment, teaching and learning, 2ed
Gavin Reid
2012/pb: 978-0-415-60758-2

Promoting and Delivering School-to-School Support for Special Educational Needs: A practical guide for SENCOs
Rita Cheminais
2013/pb 978-0-415-63370-3

Time to Talk: Implementing outstanding practice in speech, language and communication
Jean Gross
2013/pb: 978-0-415-63334-5

Curricula for Teaching Children and Young People with Severe or Profound and Multiple Learning Difficulties: Practical strategies for educational professionals
Peter Imray and Viv Hinchcliffe
2013/pb: 978-0-415-83847-4

Successfully Managing ADHD: A handbook for SENCOs and teachers
Fintan O'Regan
2014/pb: 978-0-415-59770-8

Brilliant Ideas for Using ICT in the Inclusive Classroom, 2ed
Sally McKeown and Angela McGlashon
2015/pb: 978-1-138-80902-4

3 0036 01275 9468

Boosting Learning in the Primary Classroom: Occupational therapy strategies that really work with pupils
Sheilagh Blyth
2015/pb: 978-1-13-882678-6

Beating Bureaucracy in Special Educational Needs, 3ed
Jean Gross
2015/pb: 978-1-138-89171-5

Transforming Reading Skills in the Secondary School: Simple strategies for improving literacy
Pat Guy
2015/pb: 978-1-138-89272-9

Supporting Children with Speech and Language Difficulties, 2ed
Cathy Allenby, Judith Fearon-Wilson, Sally Merrison and Elizabeth Morling
2015/pb: 978-1-138-85511-3

Supporting Children with Dyspraxia and Motor Co-ordination Difficulties, 2ed
Susan Coulter, Lesley Kynman, Elizabeth Morling, Rob Grayson and Jill Wing
2015/pb: 978-1-138-85507-6

Developing Memory Skills in the Primary Classroom: A complete programme for all
Gill Davies
2015/pb: 978-1-138-89262-0

Language for Learning in the Primary School: A practical guide for supporting pupils with language and communication difficulties across the curriculum, 2ed
Sue Hayden and Emma Jordan
2015/pb: 978-1-138-89862-2

Supporting Children with Autistic Spectrum Disorders, 2ed
Elizabeth Morling and Colleen O'Connell
2016/pb: 978-1-138-85514-4

Understanding and Supporting Pupils with Moderate Learning Difficulties in the Secondary School: A practical guide
Rachael Hayes and Pippa Whittaker
2016/pb: 978-1-138-01910-2

Assessing Children with Specific Learning Difficulties: A teacher's practical guide
Gavin Reid, Gad Elbeheri and John Everatt
2016/pb: 978-0-415-67027-2

Supporting Children with Down's Syndrome, 2ed
Lisa Bentley, Ruth Dance, Elizabeth Morling, Susan Miller and Susan Wong
2016/pb: 978-1-138-91485-8

Provision Mapping and the SEND Code of Practice: Making it work in primary, secondary and special schools, 2ed
Anne Massey
2016/pb: 978-1-138-90707-2

Supporting Children with Medical Conditions, 2ed
Susan Coulter, Lesley Kynman, Elizabeth Morling, Francesca Murray, Jill Wing and Rob Grayson
2016/pb: 978-1-13-891491-9

Supporting Children with Down's Syndrome

Second edition

Lisa Bentley, Ruth Dance, Elizabeth Morling, Susan Miller and Susan Wong

LONDON AND NEW YORK

Helping Everyone Achieve

Second edition published 2016
by Routledge
2 Park Square, Milton Park, Abingdon, Oxon OX14 4RN

and by Routledge
711 Third Avenue, New York, NY 10017

Routledge is an imprint of the Taylor & Francis Group, an informa business

© 2016 L. Bentley, R. Dance, E. Morling, S. Miller and S. Wong

The right of L. Bentley, R. Dance, E. Morling, S. Miller and S. Wong to be identified as authors of this work has been asserted by them in accordance with sections 77 and 78 of the Copyright, Designs and Patents Act 1988.

All rights reserved. The purchase of this copyright material confers the right on the purchasing institution to photocopy pages which bear the photocopy icon and copyright line at the bottom of the page. No other parts of this book may be reprinted or reproduced or utilised in any form or by any electronic, mechanical, or other means, now known or hereafter invented, including photocopying and recording, or in any information storage or retrieval system, without permission in writing from the publishers.

Trademark notice: Product or corporate names may be trademarks or registered trademarks, and are used only for identification and explanation without intent to infringe.

First edition published 2004 by David Fulton Publishers

British Library Cataloguing-in-Publication Data
A catalogue record for this book is available from the British Library

Library of Congress Cataloging in Publication Data
Supporting children with Down's syndrome / Lisa Bentley, Ruth Dance and Elizabeth Morling. – 2nd edition.
pages cm
1. Down syndrome–Patients–Education–Great Britain. 2. Children with mental disabilities–Education–Great Britain. 3. Learning disabled children–Education–Great Britain. I. Dance, Ruth. II. Morling, Elizabeth. III. Title.
LC4636.G7B46 2016
371.920941–dc23
2015007786

ISBN: 978-1-138-91482-7 (hbk)
ISBN: 978-1-138-91485-8 (pbk)
ISBN: 978-1-315-69062-9 (ebk)

Typeset in Helvetica LT Std
by Cenveo Publisher Services

Printed in Great Britain by Ashford Colour Press Ltd., Gosport, Hampshire

MIX
Paper from
responsible sources
FSC
www.fsc.org FSC® C011748

Contents

Foreword

This book was originally produced in partnership with the following services based in Hull, the Special Educational Needs Support Service, the City Educational Psychological Service and the Hull and District Down's Syndrome Association. It was written by:

Susan Miller: City Educational Psychological Service
Elizabeth Morling: (SENSS)
Susan Wong: Hull and District Down's Syndrome Association

With grateful thanks to the UK Education Consortium for Children with Down's Syndrome.

It is one of a series of books providing an up-to-date overview of special educational needs for SENCOs, teachers and other professionals and parents.

This book has now been updated to reflect current legislation and practice by:

Lisa Bentley: Educational Consultant, Downright Special Education
Ruth Dance: Educational Psychologist, Hull Learning Services
Elizabeth Morling: SEN Consultant, series editor.

Part I

Introduction

What is inclusion?

1 Inclusion in education

Inclusion can be demonstrated in a number of ways.

- It recognises that all pupils have different abilities and experiences and seeks to value and gain from these differences. It is not about expecting or trying to make everyone the same or behave in the same way.
- Education involves the process of increasing the participation of students in and reducing their exclusion from the cultures, curricula and communities of local schools.
- It involves restructuring the cultures, policies and practices in schools so that they respond to the diversity of students in their locality.
- It identifies the specific learning strengths of any particular pupil.
- It is concerned with the learning and participation of all students who are vulnerable to exclusionary pressures, not only those with impairments or those who are categorised as having 'special educational needs'.
- It views diversity not as a problem to overcome but as a rich resource to support the learning of all.

> Successful inclusion is a key step towards enabling children with Down's syndrome to become full and contributing members of the community, and society as a whole benefits... All pupils gain an understanding of diversity, disability and tolerance through being part of an inclusive school community
> (All Party Parliamentary Group on Down Syndrome 2012)

2 The legislation and guidance

The following legislation gives support to the pupil's full inclusion into a school or academy setting:

The 2014 SEND Code of Practice defines special educational needs (SEN)':

- A child or young person has SEN if they have a learning difficulty or disability that calls for special educational provision to be made for them. A child of compulsory school age or a young person has a learning difficulty or disability if they:

  (a) have a significantly greater difficulty in learning than the majority of others of the same age; or

  (b) have a disability that prevents or hinders them from making use of educational facilities of a kind generally provided for others of the same age in mainstream schools or mainstream post-16 institutions.

The 2014 SEND Code of Practice defines areas of special educational need:

Special educational needs and provision can be considered as falling under four broad areas.

1 Communication and interaction
2 Cognition and learning
3 Social, mental and emotional health
4 Sensory and/or physical

Many children and young people have difficulties that fit clearly into one of these areas; some have needs that span two or more areas.

This clearly applies to pupils with Down's syndrome.

Definition of disability under the Equality Act, 2010 defines

a person as being disabled if they have a physical or mental impairment that has a 'substantial' and 'long-term' negative effect on their ability to do normal daily activities.

Disability rights

It is against the law for a school or other education provider to treat disabled pupils/ students unfavourably. This includes:

- 'direct discrimination', e.g. refusing admission to a pupil because of a disability;
- 'indirect discrimination';
- 'discrimination arising from a disability', e.g. preventing a pupil from taking part in a school visit because of their disability;
- 'harassment', e.g. addressing a student inappropriately because they have not understood an instruction due to their disability;
- 'victimisation', e.g. suspending a disabled pupil because they have complained about harassment.

Reasonable adjustments

An educational provider has a duty to make 'reasonable adjustments' to ensure that disabled students are not discriminated against. These changes could include:

- **changes to physical features:** installing ramps to allow access to the building, classrooms;
- **providing extra support and aids:** specialist teaching and/or equipment, e.g. appropriate seating, ICT equipment.

Teachers' Standards, Department for Education, 2012

A teacher must:

Set goals that stretch and challenge pupils of all backgrounds, abilities and dispositions

Adapt teaching to respond to the strengths and needs of all pupils

- know when and how to differentiate appropriately, using approaches which enable pupils to be taught effectively;
- have a clear understanding of the needs of all pupils, including those with special educational needs; those of high ability; those with special educational needs; those with English as an additional language; those with disabilities; and be able to use and evaluate distinctive teaching approaches to engage and support them.

Make accurate and productive use of assessment

- Know and understand how to assess the relevant subject and curriculum areas, including statutory assessments.

Fulfil wider professional responsibilities

- Deploy support staff effectively.
- Communicate effectively with parents with regard to pupils' achievements and well-being.

3 Including the pupil with Down's syndrome

Education for all pupils should be a positive experience. Pupils with Down's syndrome succeed in mainstream schools for a number of reasons:

- Research shows that pupils do better academically when working in inclusive settings.
- Daily opportunities to mix with typically developing peers provide models for normal and age-appropriate behaviour.
- Pupils have opportunities to develop relationships with pupils from their own community.
- Attending mainstream school is a key step towards inclusion in the life of the community and society as a whole.
- Successful inclusion is a key step towards preparing pupils with special educational needs to become full and contributing members of the community, and society as a whole.
- Other pupils gain an understanding about disability, tolerance and how to care for and support other pupils with special needs.

Factors for inclusion to succeed:

- the determination to make it a positive experience;
- the attitude of the whole school should reflect this;
- a positive attitude solves problems;
- schools require a clear and sensitive policy on inclusion;
- senior management should support their staff and provide training to develop their skills to meet the needs of their pupils;
- in order to achieve the above they should proactively seek advice from specialist external support services, e.g. speech and language services and advisory teachers with a specific knowledge of Down's syndrome;
- good home/school liaison should be developed.

Part II

Including the pupil with Down's syndrome

4   Characteristics

Down's syndrome is one of the most common forms of learning disability: about 1 in every 1000 live births a year. It is caused by the presence of an extra copy of chromosome 21. This is known as a trisomy. Instead of the usual 46 chromosomes, a person with Down's syndrome has 47.

It is equally prevalent across all races, gender and social economic groups.

About 2–4 per cent of those with Down's syndrome have mosaic Down's syndrome. In these cases, only some of the cells in the body have the extra chromosome 21 and individuals are therefore more mildly affected and have less obvious features. The degree of difficulties for these pupils depends on the number of cells that are affected by the trisomy.

An overview of characteristics of pupils with Down's syndrome

- There is **some degree of learning difficulty** from mild to severe.
- Physical difficulties will impact on the pupil's **ability to access the curriculum**.
- Pupils will experience some degree of **health problems**.
- **Environmental factors** play an important part in development as well as genetic factors.
- **Pupils vary** as widely in their development and progress as do typically developing pupils.
- Pupils with Down's syndrome **develop more slowly than their peers**, arriving at each stage of development at a later age and staying there for longer. The developmental gap between pupils with Down's syndrome and their peers may widen with age.
- Their skills **will continue to develop** through life.

---

5   Possible medical problems

There are certain medical problems that are more prevalent in pupils with Down's syndrome. However, they are not unique to those with Down's syndrome and also appear in the rest of the population.

The problems may include:

- 40–50 per cent of those born with Down's syndrome have heart problems, half of which require heart surgery;
- an increased tendency to auto-immune conditions such as leukaemia;
- joint problems, especially arthritis;
- a significant number of pupils with Down's syndrome have hearing and visual problems;
- some pupils have a thyroid disorder;
- pupils may have a poor immune system;
- some pupils will have respiratory problems, frequent coughs and colds;
- some pupils may experience obstruction of the gastrointestinal tract;
- constipation is common due to low muscle tone in the bowel.

The above may result in pupils having significant absences from school. Each episode of illness will probably last longer than for other pupils with the same illness. After an episode of illness it will be necessary to revisit skills previously learnt.

The Down's Syndrome Association has produced a series of advisory booklets giving advice on all health conditions. These are available in print or online. Specialist advice is also available from the community paediatric nurses who have a specialism in Down's syndrome.

School staff should also seek information and advice from parents/carers.

The document 'Supporting pupils at school with a medical need in schools' 2014, will give guidance to schools, if support is required for a pupil due to medical needs.

6 The specific learning profile for Down's syndrome

Pupils with Down's syndrome are not just generally delayed in their development, they also have a specific learning profile with characteristic strengths and weaknesses. These characteristics, in conjunction with individual needs and variations within that profile, need to be considered.

Factors that may facilitate learning for pupils with Down's syndrome

Strong visual and kinaesthetic learning skills include:

- the ability to learn and use sign, gesture and visual support;
- the ability to learn and use the written word;
- the ability to learn well from demonstration and visual resources;
- the ability to learn using practical curriculum material and hands-on activities;
- the ability to copy the behaviour and attitudes of peers and adults.

Children are also highly socially motivated and empathetic towards others.

Factors that may inhibit learning for pupils with Down's syndrome:

- impaired cognitive functioning;
- delayed fine and gross motor skills;
- hearing and visual impairment;
- speech and language impairment;
- short-term auditory memory deficit;
- shorter concentration span;
- difficulties with consolidation and retention;
- difficulties with generalisation and reasoning;
- sequencing difficulties;
- avoidance strategies.

Many of the following strategies to support pupils with Down's syndrome will be recognisable as good teaching practice and so will be equally suitable for other pupils in school.

7 Classroom practice

The pupil with Down's syndrome should be treated as an individual, as a personality in his/her own right. Good classroom practice is appropriate for these pupils. However, it will be necessary to make certain considerations in order for a pupil to fully develop their potential.

- Increase structure and guidance in early years settings; the breadth of choice on offer and open-ended timescales can pose difficulties for the child.
- Consider the pupil's level of learning development – it may not be in line with their chronological age.
- Have high expectations for behaviour that are clearly communicated and constantly praised.
- Consider the appropriateness of whole-class teaching where high levels of auditory information and significant language input takes place. Delayed language skills will limit the pupil's access to the teacher's input and instructions.
- Provide visual input for the pupil in the above situation, e.g. cue cards, concrete objects, demonstrations of tasks that will support the language difficulties.
- Ensure that equipment meets the pupil's stage of development.
- It may be appropriate for older pupils with Down's syndrome to listen to a differentiated class input for a short time and then withdraw from the main group to carry out a differentiated task related to the input.
- Be aware that the classroom environment can inhibit access for those with short stature, i.e. furniture, equipment, handles that are too high or too large. Get external advice where necessary, e.g. from a service supporting pupils with a physical disability.
- Encourage co-operative working with more able peers, being aware that the pupil with Down's syndrome has a lot to contribute.
- Place the pupil with articulate peers to give good models.
- Consider when the pupil should work in a whole-class situation, in a small group or in a one-to-one situation (inclusion is the ideal).
- Give the pupil with Down's syndrome the same amount of teacher input as other pupils.
- Pupils with Down's syndrome are very successful social communicators and are acutely aware of non-verbal communication. Therefore positive body language is essential.
- Pupils with Down's syndrome are very sensitive to failure and will opt out of tasks deemed to be too difficult. Activities should be scaffolded in such a way as to be errorless and focused on teaching not testing.

- Acknowledge the level of effort required to achieve a task and give praise for tasks that are successfully completed.
- Include the pupil through a multi-sensory approach, e.g. through the use of interactive whiteboards, role play, objects related to the topic at the pupil's level of development.
- Inform all staff of the expectations for the pupil, e.g. lunchtime supervisors, parent helpers, to ensure consistency for the pupil, which will prevent 'babying' or inappropriate behaviour occurring.
- Ensure that information about the pupil is conveyed to all staff that have contact with the pupil.
- Pass on all information about the pupil, at end-of-year changes, including strategies that succeeded, in order to capitalise and build on good practice.

8 Differentiation

Teachers are responsible and accountable for the progress and development of the pupils in their class, even where pupils access support from teaching assistants or specialist staff. The class or subject teacher should remain responsible for working with the child on a daily basis. Where the interventions involve group or one-to-one teaching away from the main class or subject teacher, they should still retain responsibility for the pupil, working closely with any teaching assistants or specialist staff involved, to plan and assess the impact of interventions. The SENCO should support the class or subject teacher in the further assessment of the child's particular strengths and weaknesses, in problem solving and advising on the effective implementation of the support.

(2014 SEND Code of Practice)

Pupils with Down's syndrome will need their work differentiated in order for them to access the curriculum. They should have access to all aspects of the curriculum presented in an appropriate manner.

There are a number of ways in which differentiation can take place:

- Take into account the learning profile of the pupil with Down's syndrome and the factors within it, which will have physical and cognitive implications.
- Provide work at the appropriate stage of development.
- Start with a task, which created success on the previous day, before giving a new task. Work with a small palette of familiarly presented tasks. This reduces the dependency on decoding language in order to engage with the task. Even if the content is new, the more familiar the equipment and the approach, the more confident and comfortable the pupil will be. Pupils with Down's syndrome are very sensitive to failure or fear of failure and non-compliance is less likely to occur if the above is considered.
- Use lots of smaller, short activities, which build up to the session objective, rather than longer open-ended tasks.
- Focus on a specific objective within a curriculum topic, e.g. when working on the Crimean War, it may be appropriate for the pupil simply to know that Florence Nightingale was a nurse and that nurses look after people. It is not appropriate inclusion for the pupil to have support with the timeline cutting and sticking activity that everyone else may be doing, as they will not understand the time objective of the activity.

14

- Break all skills down into small steps.
- Use concrete objects to support work when other pupils may be working in the abstract, e.g. when talking about Florence Nightingale, have pictures, a nurse's uniform available.
- Ensure equipment is appropriate to the pupil's level of development, e.g. 'Numicon' for maths lessons may still be required in key stage 2.
- Give support in practical sessions where manipulation of equipment may be difficult, e.g. tools in technology lessons, science apparatus. Use equipment of the correct size, e.g. small looped scissors, saws with small handles.
- Use assessment publications to find the appropriate level of work, e.g. 'BSquared', 'PIVATS'.
- Use descriptors for previous key stages.
- Allow time for planning and liaison between staff and to prepare and differentiate materials.

9 Visual impairment

Many pupils with Down's syndrome have some sort of visual impairment. All children have poor visual acuity, resulting in slightly blurred vision at a close range of 25 cm. In addition, 60–70 per cent of children before the age of seven, require glasses for other refractive problems. Bifocals are routinely recommended.

Pupils can also be highly visually distractible and may struggle to concentrate in busy visual environments.

Strategies to support the pupil

- Place the pupil near the front of the class.
- Ensure that the pupil can see the whiteboard or storybook.
- A copy of information from the electronic whiteboard or PowerPoints should be at the side of the pupil; programs exist that can transfer documents directly onto tablets, which the pupil can hand hold.
- Ensure the pupil is seated with minimal visual distraction, e.g. away from window, at the front, using a workstation.
- Use larger bold type – 24+ at all times.
- Use simple, clear presentation on worksheets, with an unfussy font of appropriate size.
- Use an angle board.
- Ensure print size and spacing in reading books is appropriate as the pupil rises through stages of the reading scheme.
- Use a reading ruler or a card with a gap to track words.
- Consider the use of larger squared paper in mathematics.
- Enlarge the font size on the computer screen; check the colour of the background screen is the clearest for the pupil to read.
- Give pens with thicker nibs, which produce writing that is easier to see.
- Ensure that the pupil wears spectacles if prescribed.
- Use enlarged material, when the pupil is being assessed, whether internally or externally.
- Seek advice from the specialist visual impairment service involved with the pupil.

10 Hearing impairment

Many pupils with Down's syndrome experience some hearing loss especially in the early years. Levels of hearing can vary from day to day. Some 15 per cent of pupils have sensori-neural hearing loss that is permanent. It is necessary to determine whether hearing difficulties or poor understanding of language cause a lack of response. Poor auditory processing and poor auditory memory contribute to difficulty with understanding. Therefore discriminating between similar sounds, and the learning and use of phonics is likely to be problematic.

Strategies to support hearing difficulties

- Place the pupil near the front of the class.
- Gain the pupil's attention before speaking.
- Face the pupil when speaking to him/her.
- Reinforce speech with signs, gestures and encouragement to watch other pupils.
- Support phonic knowledge with a pictorial scheme e.g. 'Jolly Phonics', 'Read Write Inc.' or 'See and Learn: Playing with Sounds'.
- Give other prompts – pictures, prompts in a written form.
- Repeat other pupils' responses.
- Repeat instructions to the pupil after the whole group input, to ensure understanding.
- Encourage independent learning by giving a simple, written or pictorial task list with a motivating reward at the end.
- Seek advice from the hearing impairment service, if appropriate.

11 Transition from primary to secondary school

A number of considerations need to be made as the pupil makes the transition from primary to secondary school.

- The choice of a receiving school with a positive attitude.
- A carefully prepared transition plan, which is drawn up at the annual review, held in the final year of primary school. This should involve:

  - the teachers, SENCOs and support assistants from the primary school and the secondary school;
  - professionals from outside agencies, e.g. educational psychologists, speech and language therapists;
  - parents;
  - views of the pupil.

  The plan should consider:

  - visits from secondary school staff to the pupil in the primary school to discover the strengths of the pupil and successful strategies;
  - additional visits to the receiving school for the pupil;
  - home/school communication;
  - management of support; on transitions around school, in the learning environment and at non-structured times;
  - access to the curriculum and how differentiation will take place;
  - transfer of the pupil's learning profile, i.e. the levels of attainment, appropriate learning methods, language skills, areas of strength and difficulty;
  - personal profile of the pupil with contributions from the primary school, parents and friends.

- A communication passport should be devised that reflects the above with contributions from the pupil, e.g. 'I need…, I'm good at reading, I don't like…'
- Staff training should be put into place: about Down's syndrome (from a specialist Down's syndrome advisor), the pupil's learning profile, differentiation.
- The appropriate use of adult support (possibly more than one worker) should be discussed, in order to support subjects and promote independence.
- Consideration should be given to the pupil's stamina related to schools on large sites – this may require support. This could be timetabling of tutorial groups in a ground-floor room, use of lifts.
- Support for the pupil to learn new routines, understand new expectations for behaviour, learn the layout of the school and transition from one lesson to another, will be necessary.

- Support may be required for functional independence (personal hygiene routines, dressing after PE and organising themselves in the dining hall).
- Consideration should be given to organisation at unstructured times, e.g. break and lunchtimes.
- Peer group integration may require support through encouragement to join clubs, buddy systems, Circle of Friends.
- Development of understanding of the nature of Down's syndrome through PSHE (personal, social, health and economic education).
- Medical conditions may require extra support outlined within an Individual Health Care Plan.
- Effective parent partnership is essential for the pupil to settle into a new school and good communication is important for joint strategies to take place. It should be acknowledged that not all parents have the confidence to communicate easily with a secondary school and strategies will be required to overcome this, e.g. a member of staff from the primary school could accompany the parents on a school visit, having previously discussed any concerns of the parents. They may also support the parent in subsequent meetings. Support from a parent partnership organisation may also provide support.
- Homework will need to be recorded in a diary and the amount given may need to be reduced in quantity.

Further information can be gained from the Down's Syndrome Association.

Part III

Use of support staff for the pupil with Down's syndrome

12 Adult support for the pupil

Pupils with Down's syndrome will require some level of additional adult support to cover the following areas:

- encouraging independence;
- developing language skills;

  - signing;
  - implementing a speech and language programme devised by a speech and language therapist;
  - promoting good listening skills.

- developing confidence;
- developing self-esteem;
- developing social interaction;

  - supporting peers to include the pupil with Down's syndrome.

- developing co-operative working;
- developing independence;

  - hygiene;
  - dressing;
  - eating;
  - independent movement around the site.

- supporting access to the curriculum;

  - delivering differentiated material devised by the teacher;
  - making additional materials;
  - simplifying instructions;
  - providing visual clues;
  - providing alternative recording methods.

- ensuring all equipment is available, e.g. laptops are charged up in readiness for a lesson.

13 Support staff
Effective deployment

Teachers standards 2012 states that teaching staff should:

'Fulfil wider professional responsibilities by deploying support staff effectively.'

> All pupils with Down's syndrome are likely to require additional adult support at some level in order to access the curriculum.
>
> Effective deployment does not necessarily mean that the pupil has constant one-to-one support.

The 2014 SEND Code of Practice states:

> Where the interventions involve group or one-to-one teaching away from the main class or subject teacher, they should **still retain responsibility for the pupil**, working closely with any teaching assistants or specialist staff involved, **to plan and assess the impact of interventions**.

Teachers may consider the following issues to ensure the most effective deployment of support staff:

- Support staff should promote independence at all times.
- It will not be necessary to work alongside the pupil in every lesson.
- Consider the seating position of support staff within the classroom. Ensure positioning of staff does not prevent the pupil from being included in and accessing the lesson.
- The pupil should look to the teacher and not be reliant on the teaching assistant. The pupil may need this to be made explicit. A visual cue could be used, e.g. the pupil wears a badge with a relevant photo, saying 'I am listening to Mrs Jones', or whoever is the adult focus. The adult wears a badge, again with accompanying photo, saying 'Johanna is listening to me'.
- Support staff should take notes during teacher input in order to reinforce key points at a later stage in the lesson.
- Support staff should monitor and record appropriate information about the pupil, e.g. work output, temperament. The level of support given should also be noted to allow accurate assessments to take place.

- Liaison procedures between home and school should be established under the guidance of the SENCO/Head of Year/Class Teacher or Form Tutor.
- Support staff should work under the direction of the SENCO, class teacher or individual subject teachers to ensure an accurate picture of the pupil's progress is shown.
- In practical sessions when the pupil needs to manipulate specialised equipment, support staff should work under the direction of the pupil.
- Withdrawal of the pupil for programmes, such as speech and language therapy, should be negotiated with the SENCO and individual subject teachers.

14 Support staff
Roles and responsibilities

Support staff should:

Have a clear understanding of their roles and responsibilities:

- Have a knowledge of their job description.
- Maintain a professional demeanour with parents.
- Be aware of school policies with regard to behaviour, anti-bullying, child protection.
- Respect the confidentiality of information for all pupils.

Be aware of channels of communication within the school:

- Ensure that information given by parents is given to the appropriate member of staff – class teacher, SENCO.
- Ensure that communication with outside agencies is carried out in consultation with the SENCO.
- Ensure that recommendations and reports from outside agencies are passed to the teacher and SENCO.
- Ensure that information given to parents is with the knowledge of the class teacher.
- Ensure that there is a mechanism for disseminating information to support staff about school activities, e.g. daily diary, staff room notice board.

Be recognised as valued members of a team:

- Participate in the planning and monitoring process.

Be encouraged to make use of their personal skills:

- Share skills, e.g. ICT, creative skills.

Be supported with appropriate ongoing professional development:

- Observe and learn from other professionals in school and in other establishments.
- Undertake training in school and through external courses.

Encourage the pupil's independence at all times:

- Promote independent work habits.
- Promote independent life skills.
- Promote independent play skills.

15 Support staff
Guidelines for working with pupils

Avoid	but instead...
sitting next to the pupil at all times	work with other pupils, whilst keeping an eye on the pupil with Down's syndrome
offering too close an oversight during breaks and lunchtimes	encourage playing with peers, introduce games to include others if necessary
collecting equipment for the pupil or putting it away	encourage the pupil to carry this out with independence (ensure storage places are clearly marked)
completing a task for a pupil	ensure that work is at an appropriate level and is carried out with minimal support (note any support given)
allowing behaviour that is not age-appropriate to the pupil, e.g. holding hands in the playground or in school	encourage the development of more age-appropriate peer relationships by social engineering, 'buddying' or circle of friends
making unnecessary allowances for the pupil	use social stories, visual cues and rewards to help develop appropriate behaviour
tolerating inappropriate behaviour	follow the behaviour policy
making unrealistic demands on the pupil	ensure instructions and work are at the appropriate level
making decisions for the pupil	give the pupil opportunities to make choices and decisions
over-dependency on the support assistant	encourage independent behaviour and work

Part IV

Specific issues in teaching and learning for the pupil with Down's syndrome

16 Developing speech and language

Pupils with Down's syndrome have speech and language difficulties that follow a specific impairment profile. Pupils have better understanding of language (receptive skills) than their spoken ability (expressive skills) would suggest, though both show delay. In particular, pupils have significant difficulty processing auditory information and retaining it for future use.

For many, the speech and language deficits are the most significant area of difficulty. The language delay is caused by a combination of factors, some of which are physical and some due more to perceptual and cognitive problems. Research shows that the acquisition of all speech and language skills is best supported using visual means, particularly the written word.

The consequences of a delay in language acquisition may comprise:

- longer processing time for all language activities;
- difficulty learning the rules of grammar;
- the use of single key words instead of sentences;
- the omission of connecting words, prepositions;
- difficulty in asking for information or help;
- adults who answer for them or finish their sentences;
- insufficient practice to improve their clarity of speech;
- problems in learning and managing social language;
- a smaller vocabulary, which can lessen the ability to acquire general knowledge;
- problems in understanding specific language of the curriculum;
- *any delay in learning to understand and use the language is likely to lead to cognitive delay. The level of knowledge and understanding and thus the ability to access the curriculum will inevitably be affected.*

There are a number of strategies to support the development of speech and language skills.

Practising sounds (oromotor)

A smaller mouth cavity and weaker, less co-ordinated mouth and tongue muscles cause difficulty in forming words, therefore:

- Practising oromotor exercises as prescribed by the SALT is essential. This could include the Talktools programme.
- Use visual and kinaesthetic support to encourage articulation of individual sounds, e.g. 'Jolly Phonics', 'Read Write Inc.' or 'See and Learn: Playing with Sounds'.
- Consider articulation apps on tablets, e.g. 'Articulation Station'.

Listening and understanding skills

Pupils have poor auditory memory skills, which inhibits the ability to remember instructions, individual words and sentences.

- Seat near the teacher; many pupils may have a hearing impairment as well.
- Give the pupil's first name, pause and ensure their attention before speaking.
- Ensure face-to-face interaction and good eye contact with the pupil.
- Give the pupil time to process language and respond; do not repeat the instruction again too quickly.
- Use simple, familiar language and short concise sentences, in the order events will happen, e.g. 'coat on, out to play'.
- Play games where the pupil has to listen out for and follow increasing numbers of key words (information-carrying words). 'Can you wash baby's hands?' where there is a choice between a baby and teddy, wash cloth and hairbrush.
- Play sound bag games to encourage auditory discrimination skills where the pupil has to sort objects into sets according to two given sounds.
- Syllable tap familiar words and new topic words.
- Provide lots of short listening activities/games to strengthen auditory skills.
- Reinforce spoken instructions with print, pictures, diagrams, symbols and concrete materials.
- The number of instructions given should be reflective of the pupil's auditory memory capacity. The speech and language therapist will give this information.
- Check the pupil's understanding of instructions by asking them to repeat back the instruction. This is only appropriate for pupils with more expressive language.
- Avoid ambiguous vocabulary that can cause confusion, e.g. 'How high is that number?'
- Reinforce speech with sign language, facial expression and gesture.
- Emphasise key words, reinforcing in a visual manner.
- Use sign language, pictures, objects, interactive whiteboard and tablets to make all teacher input more accessible and memorable. Record ideas on a small white-board or ICT, ready for later use.
- Use the 'Talk for Writing' style approach to help with retention of stories.

Vocabulary development

Pupils learn new words steadily but can have difficulty in remembering them. Research shows that the children remember what they see therefore showing the written word from infancy helps them retain the sound of that word. Slower general development may have limited the exposure to a wide range of vocabulary so this has to be proactively taught and not assumed.

- Start to teach reading from the age of two, beginning with familiar, everyday words, e.g. own name, mummy, teddy, own special objects of interest. Programmes such as 'See and Learn First Word Pictures' and the apps 'Touch Words' and 'Special Words' support this.
- Vocabulary checklists are available, e.g. from Down Syndrome Education International, which help chart both the quantity and quality of vocabulary development.
- Pupils will not learn classroom topic vocabulary incidentally, so this will need to be pre-taught before the rest of the class embarks on the topic, if class inputs are to make any sense. This can be achieved by using a similar lotto matching board approach to that of 'See and Learn'.
- Once taught, pupils are usually good at remembering the names for objects/activities. However, what is far more challenging is knowing what the meaning of that word is (semantics). Pupils must also be explicitly taught this aspect of vocabulary and encouraged to explore words through mind mapping, grouping, sorting and odd one out activities. It is useful to add definition cards onto a lotto board once the pupil can recognise the new words.
- Label objects around the school and grounds.
- Use good clear, uncluttered non-fiction texts as reading books to support topic work; or make books covering the key vocabulary from the topic.

Grammar acquisition

Learning grammar poses particular difficulties for pupils with Down's syndrome because it is heavily dependent on memory. They are particularly prone to leaving out the small words of grammar and grammatical markers that have no clear meaning. Reading and composing written sentences are the most effective ways of supporting grammar acquisition. These can be supported with pictures and symbols where necessary.

- Use high frequency words to compose simple sentences from the earliest days using word cards, 'Clicker' or stickers with the words written on them. These could be matched to a sentence model in the first instance.
- Use signed grammar markers as a visual cue, even after the pupil has dropped other signing.
- Use a colour coded support system, e.g. 'Colourful Semantics', to help the pupil order the elements of a sentence and answer 'who', 'what', 'where' and 'when' questions.
- Follow a systematic programme to help the pupil learn to decode language, e.g. 'Language for Thinking' under the guidance of the speech and language therapist.
- Avoid closed questions and encourage the pupil to speak in more than one word utterances; extend by modelling, e.g. the pupil says 'car' and the adult extends this to 'a blue car'.
- Use apps specifically designed to support grammar acquisition, e.g. 'Sentence Builder', 'Sentence Maker', which utilise the learning style appropriate to Down's syndrome.

Expressive language

This is the most problematic area of language development for most pupils with Down's syndrome as it requires the co-ordination of all of the above. Expressive language can lag significantly behind understanding and is no real indicator of the level of cognitive ability. Expressive language includes both sign and speech.

- Signing is a bridge to speaking and encourages the development of vocabulary, grammar and thought. The pupil will automatically drop it when they can make themselves understood verbally. Ideally the whole school, otherwise all classroom members, practitioners and peers, should be a signing community where the pupil with Down's syndrome can be understood.
- Ensure the pupil has to ask for things. Use carrier sentences to support requesting and other interaction: 'Can I have…?'; 'I want…'; 'Can I play?'
- Make books that practise functional language that the child might want to use in other contexts, e.g. 'I like' book or 'My favourite things'.
- Practise social scripts that allow the pupil to join in with their peers, e.g. 'My turn now', 'Good shot' and 'I don't like it'. Some of these will also reduce unwanted behaviours.
- Rehearse information about themselves alongside the appropriate questions from the earliest days, e.g. 'My name is Jenny Smith'. Move on to cover address, birth date, age, school, likes and dislikes. The pupil must learn to communicate key information about themselves without the support of an adult.
- Use a home-school diary to prompt the pupil to share their news with parents and help adults and peers understand what the pupil is saying. Ideally supported by a photo, this should be written in the first person, e.g. 'I made a puppet of the Gruffalo'. Parents can then write in return about something the pupil has done in the home context, including photos or relevant objects from a visit. The pupil must be given the opportunity to share this within the classroom, preferably within their peer group. The app 'Special Stories' facilitates this with ease and allows the child to record themselves reading the sentence without the pressure of an audience. Clicker Stories is also useful for longer pieces.
- Encourage the pupil to speak aloud by using visual and written prompts. The pupil may find it easier to read information than to speak spontaneously.
- Allow the pupil to have prepared their answers/ideas using quick sentence construction tools such as 'Clicker' or 'Colourful Semantics' before making an oral response. This allows rehearsal of the sentence before it is spoken to an audience.
- Use a rehearsal technique (see section on Independent writing for details) to help the child remember what it is they want to say. Extend the length of utterance as the pupil's memory improves.
- Set up regular and additional opportunities to speak to others, e.g. taking and reading messages.
- Develop expressive opportunities through drama, role play, puppets and small world play.

17   Addressing behaviour issues

As with other pupils, those with Down's syndrome may display behaviour problems and may need to be taught to behave in a socially acceptable way and to respond in an appropriate manner. Due to their language difficulties, pupils with Down's syndrome may find the environment around them a little confusing and have limited verbal skills for gaining appropriate help and support. Their developmental delay may result in them exhibiting the behaviour of a younger child, but with appropriate support, the pupil will pass through the normal developmental stages, albeit at a slower pace. A greater use of structure within the school day and within activities will help prevent the onset of behavioural difficulties.

There are some basic expectations in schools that pupils are required to follow, which may need to be taught explicitly:

- an awareness of expected behaviour at certain times and in certain places, e.g. lining up, sitting appropriately in assembly;
- class and school rules;
- appropriate responses to requests and instructions;
- co-operation with others at work and play.

It may be necessary to develop strategies to address behavioural issues, which may arise:

- Adopt a highly structured environment supported by a visual timetable for the day, and within individual sessions. There are apps to support this approach.
- Be sure to analyse **why** a behaviour has occurred in the first place: there is always a reason. Use functional behaviour analysis. Asking what happened, when and who was involved, will help identify the why, and reveal patterns of behaviour, which can then be worked on.
- Use short, clear instructions appropriate to the pupil's level of understanding and support, with demonstrations of the task.
- Ensure work is at the appropriate level, taking into account all the pupil's deficit skills. Fear of failure will result in task avoidance.
- Match the length of the task to the pupil's ability to concentrate. Use lots of shorter tasks within a session, which work towards the same objective, rather than a single open-ended task.

- Pupils tire more easily, so build sessions with a mix of higher and lower demand tasks within them.
- Finish an activity on a positive note. Do not continue an activity for so long that the pupil gets tired and unco-operative. They will return to the task in a negative mood tomorrow.
- Distinguish the 'can't do' from the 'won't do'.
- Develop a range of strategies to deal with avoidance behaviours.
- Ignore attention-seeking behaviour, within reasonable limits. Withdraw and focus your attention on another pupil who is displaying the desired behaviour. Most pupils with Down's syndrome desire social interaction so much that they will then comply in order to come back into the social group.
- Unlike other pupils, those with Down's syndrome are under the constant supervision of an adult and some react badly to the loss of control this engenders. Back off and make sure the pupil is allowed to exercise choice wherever possible.
- Increasing independence alleviates behavioural issues, so approaches such as TEACCH may benefit some pupils.
- Mark change of activities using timers, bells, recordings (try using 'Talking Tins') or pictures. 'Now' and 'next' boards help pupils, where the 'now' may be the expected (but not the one necessarily desired by the pupil!) activity and the 'next' a choice activity.
- Ensure that the pupil is aware of the expectations or rules of a given situation. Frame rules in the positive. Tell him/her what to do. 'Walk slowly' not 'Don't run'.
- Encourage positive behaviour by developing good behaviour prompt pictures, e.g. tidying up or sitting appropriately.
- Use simple, reinforcing phrases every time the child complies, e.g. 'Good sitting'.
- Ensure that the pupil works with peers who can act as good role models.
- Reinforce the desired behaviour immediately with visual, oral or tangible rewards. Cumulative rewards, e.g. golden time given at the end of the week, have little meaning to a pupil with short-term memory problems.
- Any penalties or punishments should take place straight after the event and not some time later.
- Dealing with inappropriate behaviour should be a shared responsibility, not just the role of the support assistant.
- Teach new rules that apply to new situations in a very explicit way, as the pupil moves through school. Use 'Social Stories' to teach situational behaviour.
- Avoid assuming that difficulties are lodged within the pupil or are specific to Down's syndrome.
- Seek support from outside agencies, if behaviour problems cannot be addressed through school intervention.

18   Developing memory

Pupils with Down's syndrome experience poor auditory short-term memory and auditory processing skills.

> The auditory short-term memory is the memory store used to hold, process, understand and assimilate spoken language long enough to respond to it. Any deficit in short-term auditory memory will greatly affect pupils' ability to respond to the spoken word or learn from any situation entirely reliant on their auditory skills. In addition, they will find it more difficult to follow and remember verbal instructions. This also affects consolidation and retention of skills.

There are a variety of ways of improving memory skills

- Sing nursery rhymes frequently, leave a pause and let the pupil give the last word e.g. 'Humpty Dumpty sat on the…'
- Read simple stories with repetitive lines, e.g. 'the Gingerbread Man' and ask the pupil to join in the repetitions.
- Read a very simple story a few times and at strategic points ask what comes next.
- Tell jokes and silly poems, which the pupil can take home to relate to their family.
- Use chants, raps and rhymes to learn alphabetical order, days of the week, etc.
- Ask the pupil to fetch an article, build up the number of articles to be fetched over time.
- Ask the pupil to put equipment away in the correct place.
- Play 'Kim's Game' with two articles on the tray, initially, gradually increasing the number of articles.
- Use a rehearsal strategy of naming a series of pictures/words in sequence from beneath flaps.
- Use apps that practise memory and sequencing skills, e.g. 'Match and Find' (Special iApps).
- Try the 'See and Learn Memory' program.
- Talk about what is being done when a task is being carried out, e.g. during baking. Recall what has been done by asking simple questions with picture prompts using the equipment, e.g. 'What did we put in the bowl?'
- Ask the pupil to repeat what she/he has to do when instructions have been given supported by picture cue cards or written prompts on Post-its.
- Give opportunities to take messages supported by picture/written prompts.

Encourage coping strategies to overcome poor memory:

- Develop the use of cue cards, e.g. a picture that shows what is to be done, in order to supplement poor auditory memory.
- Utilise notebooks, visual timetables, homework notebooks, home-school diaries.
- Use appropriate ICT programs to help develop skills.

Always overlearn previous objectives whilst learning new ideas, otherwise previous skills and ideas will be lost.

Always accompany auditory information with visual cues, modelling and practical examples.

19 Developing mathematical skills

Pupils with Down's syndrome will probably experience difficulty in this area of the curriculum because:

- poor working memory causes difficulty following mathematical processes;
- poor auditory memory causes difficulty in remembering instructions;
- development of limited language skills may affect concept development;
- acquisition of abstract concepts may be restricted;
- poor fine motor skills will inhibit recording;
- an inability to generalise information.

It will be necessary to support the development of mathematics through a number of strategies.

- Use 'Numicon Firm Foundations' from the pre-school years, Kits 1 and 2 later.
- Use the 'See and Learn Numbers' and 'Special Numbers' app for early number recognition.
- Develop a structure within the maths lesson that encompasses a small-steps and highly structured approach.
- Recognise that the fast moving pace of the maths curriculum will be inappropriate.
- Develop an appropriate individual programme that matches the pupil's developmental level.
- Teach one concrete approach for number operations rather than a lot of different approaches.
- Recognise that mental maths will be extremely difficult and will need support with concrete objects and at an individual pace.
- Give direct teaching of component skills as they will not be gained incidentally.
- Provide opportunities for daily repetition of what has been learnt.
- Give lots of practice to consolidate learning at each stage.
- Work systematically through the number system; jumping around through the curriculum will be unhelpful and result in unlinked patchy knowledge.
- Pre-learn mathematical vocabulary: 'Makaton for Maths' should be considered.
- Learning needs to be practical and experiential in the class, e.g. cubes, number lines, Cuisenaire, Stern rods, real coins. Teach time using digital clocks to minimise language difficulties.
- Give a precise, consistent verbal description to the pupil of what is being learnt.

- Skills that have been learnt need to be generalised to other settings.
- Use alternative methods of recording answers to prevent poor motor skills hindering progress, e.g. an adult to scribe, the use of stickers with pre-written numbers, number stamps, use of a laptop/tablet with problems pre-written, apps utilising one mathematical concept.
- Provide simplified, uncluttered worksheets with an appropriate font size.
- Consider the use of ICT.

20 Developing reading skills

Pupils with Down's syndrome can become good readers, with the ability to learn to read with meaning. Reading will:

- improve language skills;
- develop the ability to think and reason;
- aid understanding;
- improve access to a variety of areas of the curriculum;
- overcome difficulties in taking understanding from the spoken language.

A number of considerations need to be taken into account in order to develop reading skills:

- It is not necessary to be 'ready to read', particularly for the pupil with poor expressive language – start sooner rather than later. The 'See and Learn' scheme is appropriate from about the age of two.
- Use a whole word approach to build up sight vocabulary; using phonics as a primary approach is inappropriate due to difficulties with auditory memory, accurate hearing, discrimination of sounds and problem solving skills.
- However, a phonic programme should be developed in a differentiated manner using onset and rime to develop blending skills.
- Teach functional words initially that are relevant to the pupil, e.g. mum, dad, baby, teddy, cat and dog.
- Individual words should be taught using lotto boards and matching word cards, as in the 'See and Learn' scheme published by Down Syndrome Education International.
- Use the above words linked to photographs to make the pupil's first books, using a progression; single word, e.g. 'baby', then include a verb 'baby is sleeping', then put in a proposition 'teddy is on the table'. 'See and Learn' works through such a progression.
- Consider an alternative to speech for a pre-verbal pupil, e.g. the pupil signs the words so that the development of reading can progress.
- Use a structured non-phonic reading scheme, e.g. 'PM Starters', which gradually introduces high frequency words. A Down's syndrome specific scheme, 'POPS', is also available.

- Also any commercial reading scheme that uses a core vocabulary could be successfully used by adopting the 'See and Learn' approach.
- Supplement commercial schemes with a customised reading scheme, to provide a very structured approach, which could be linked to the pupil's interest.
- Ensure pupils are able to understand what they read, as limited language skills can result in decoding rather than reading with understanding in later years.
- Label objects within the environment.
- Utilise simple written sentences to support all other areas of the curriculum, e.g. written instructions, timetables, simple instructions on worksheets, prompt lists, all of which will also support independence.
- Produce topic-related reading books and lotto boards to support other curriculum areas.
- Generalise words learnt to other situations, e.g. look for words in the environment, attach notes to objects with familiar words for the pupil to read, e.g. 'this is my book'.
- Give the pupil time to think before prompting.
- Recognise that overlearning will be necessary to consolidate skills that have been learnt. The overarching 'A Reading and Language Intervention for Children with Down Syndrome' document is available from Down Syndrome Education International.

21 Developing independent writing

Pupils with Down's syndrome may take longer to develop independent writing skills because of difficulties with:

- short-term auditory and working memory;
- speech and language skills;
- fine motor skills;
- organising and sequencing information;
- sequencing events;
- sequencing words into a sentence.

Pupils with Down's syndrome can be supported to develop independent writing skills in a number of ways:

(Importantly, when developing writing skills it is essential that the pencil is not regarded as the main tool for recording work, therefore, 'writing' in the following chapter refers to the use of ICT in preference but not necessarily to the exclusion of the pencil.)

- Emergent writing is not the appropriate approach to developing independent writing; a more structured method that integrates the use of high frequency and topic words is advisable.
- Develop keyboard skills, using a 'Big Keys' keyboard with lower case keys, from an early age.
- Capitalise on reading skills by using a word bank (limit the number of words included) and a sentence stand to build sentences using vocabulary learnt whilst developing reading.
- Use the 'Clicker' programs on a computer or tablet using key words that the pupil can read.
- Develop sentence starts on cards, for the pupil to copy and finish, e.g. 'Here is a …', 'I can see the …' using words developed in the reading vocabulary. Encourage the pupil to use these sentence starts in an independent manner.
- Practise remembering a sentence by:

  1 verbalising rehearsal using actions;
  2 presenting a sentence on individual word cards to read;
  3 concealing individual cards face down in order;

4   asking the pupil to give the sentence back rehearsing one word at a time –
    pupil reinserts **first** word from memory, followed by **first** and **second**, then
    first, **second**, **third** and so on;
5   recording the sentence (orally onto any recording device).

- Provide visual prompts to develop independence:

    - word cards using words the pupil already knows;
    - picture cues to support the structure of a story;
    - desktop charts with everyday words; colours, days of the week;
    - story frames;
    - key word prompts to support story writing.

- Provide sequencing activities, e.g. sequencing cards showing activities during the day.
- Refer to the home/school diary to help the pupil recall familiar events to write about.
- Provide concrete experiences to discuss and describe in his/her writing.
- Use recording to support the development of grammar.
- Provide alternative methods of recording the pupil's ideas:

    - scribe;
    - cloze procedure;
    - a series of pictures to tell a story, e.g. from a visit, accompanied by captions, written by the pupil or adult;
    - record the pupil recounting his/her story, which can then be transcribed by an adult;
    - use of 'Special Stories' app;
    - ICT equipment.

22 Teaching spelling

Pupils with Down's syndrome will learn to spell mainly from visual memory.

Delayed speech and language skills and poor auditory and working memory will cause difficulties when learning to spell words phonically. Pupils need to learn to spell early in their school careers in order to have the basic tools available for independent writing.

A number of suggestions need to be taken into account to help with the acquisition of spellings.

- It is not essential for a pupil to be able to accurately articulate a word before the spelling of it is taught.
- Although a phonic approach to spelling is not initially appropriate for pupils with Down's syndrome, a visual and kinaesthetic scheme such as 'Jolly Phonics' or 'Read Write Inc.' should be used to teach phonemes.
- Ensure the pupil can read and understand the words to be learnt.
- Be realistic about the number of spellings being taught and revise regularly.
- Teach words that will promote speech and language development.
- Develop a very structured spelling programme, which allows for progress in small steps. This should teach both high frequency words and word family groups concurrently.
- Word families should initially be taught using onset and rime, e.g. c-at, m-at, r-at, until the pupil's auditory memory span improves. The pattern and order of the letter groups can be reinforced by using colour coding and manual equipment such as magnetic letters and multi-phonic bricks.
- Teach words that the pupil will use frequently in their own writing.
- Greater success will be achieved by working through two- and three-letter words before moving onto longer words.
- Practise spellings in a kinaesthetic way, e.g. finger tracing, writing in sand, magnetic letters, multi-phonic bricks.
- Use the look–cover–write–check method.
- Pupils should have frequent practice at using their new spelling knowledge, both HFW and phonic, in written sentences, not using a pencil but ICT equipment instead.
- Explore spelling activities on the computer or tablet.

- Teach words or have them available on a word list (with a picture cue) that are required for specific subjects being covered, e.g. to fit a history topic.
- Reinforce meanings of abstract words with symbols or signs.
- Provide a word bank with pictures to reinforce meaning – arrange alphabetically.
- Use picture dictionaries in preference to 'normal' dictionaries.

23 Fine and gross motor skills

All pupils with Down's syndrome have poor muscle tone, loose joints, slack liga-
ments and short stubby fingers, which affect their fine and gross motor skills.
Most have problems developing appropriate balance. Pupils will fatigue more
quickly than their peers.

**There are a number of strategies that can be implemented, as the pupil
progresses, to develop gross and fine motor skills.**

Gross motor skills

- Encourage a wide range of outdoor play at home and school.
- Adopt a staged approach to developing gross motor skills in a hierarchical manner,
  i.e. improve balance, then running, jumping, hopping through appropriate activities, some of which can be found in 'Ready, Steady go to PE!'
- Encourage full participation in all aspects of PE with differentiated activities and
  the use of relevant language and demonstration using the right orientation.
- Suitable equipment will support differentiation, e.g., balls with extra attachments to
  catch, soft large foam balls, short-handled racquets/bats.

Fine motor skills

- Pre-writing skills should be started in the early years and need to continue for a
  longer time than is needed by most of their peers. The following describes the
  necessary skills that would be relevant together with appropriate activities:

  - finger isolation, e.g. popping bubbles, finger puppets;
  - using two hands together activities, e.g. holding a bowl whilst stirring, thread-
    ing beads (start with large beads onto a dowel, then a bead with a large hole
    onto a nylon washing line, then onto a lace with a stiffened end), peeling a
    banana;
  - wrist-strengthening activities, e.g. screw toys, opening screw tops, sharpening
    pencils;
  - finger-strengthening activities, e.g. rolling, tracing, drawing, cutting, squeezing
    and building;

- encourage a pincer grip by picking up small items, squeezing spring pegs, picking up objects with teabag tongs, taking out raisins from an ice cube tray using finger and thumb, sorting small objects.

- Develop keyboard skills from an early age:
  - first learn to type the name using a model;
  - type without a model (it may be necessary to do this by building up one letter at a time;
  - use appropriate typing programs, e.g. BBC 'Dance Mat' (downloaded from the Internet);
  - use 'Big Keys' keyboards, a specialist mouse, e.g. a roller ball mouse, a small mouse.

Handwriting will be difficult to develop but the following should be considered:

- Be aware of the order of skill development, i.e. the pupil should be able to produce certain shapes before handwriting is introduced:

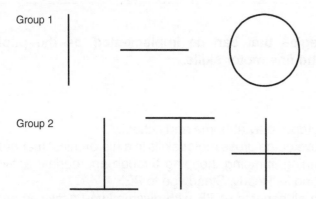

Group 1

Group 2

- Develop the above patterns in a multi-sensory way:
  - pushing a car (left to right) across a 'race track';
  - make patterns with wet paintbrushes, playground chalks;
  - make patterns between tramlines of decreasing size with large felt tip pens, crayons;
  - use fingers in the sand to trace over writing patterns;
  - join dots on a whiteboard.
- Consider the use of the 'Write from the Start' programme to develop writing and perceptual skills (it may be necessary to enlarge the photocopied sheets).
- Use a structured handwriting scheme (printing will be easier than joined script). Use apps to develop letter formation. 'Letter School' utilises an errorless, multisensory approach.
- Ensure furniture is at the correct height for the pupil, to allow concentration on the task rather than balancing. Provide smaller tables, with chairs that allow the pupil to place their elbows comfortably on the table.
- Footblocks will allow their feet to rest on a surface and a sloping board will provide a comfortable working position.

- Specialised or modified equipment may be needed, e.g. short-handled paint-brushes, inset puzzles with large knobs, triangular pencils and pens, pencil grips, e.g. 'Crossguard' grips, small spring scissors (see Appendices for suppliers).
- Avoid copying from the blackboard: give 'PowerPoint' notes and pre-drawn diagrams to be labelled.
- Provide alternative recording methods of recording the pupil's ideas, i.e. scribing, use of recording equipment, e.g. a dictaphone, tablet.
- Specialist equipment may be required for science and technology, e.g. an auto chopper, food processor for mixing, lightweight tools, clamps to hold wood when sawing. Adult support may be required to aid the use of equipment and ensure safety.

Further information to develop fine motor skills can be found in the publication *Writing Handwriting* (see Resources section).

24 The use of ICT

> The delay in fine motor development can hinder the pupil's cognitive development and limit the amount of practice they get in composing their own work.
>
> As visual learners with accompanying sensory impairment, pupils with Down's syndrome require all information to be presented visually, therefore ICT offers the best access to the curriculum.
>
> ICT uses the automatic part of the brain that is less impaired and utilises skills that children have already been developing within the home, e.g. parents' phones, tablets, laptops.

The use of technology will benefit pupils in a variety of ways.

- ICT reduces the difficulties related to the use of fine motor equipment and should be the alternative to using a pencil in all areas of the curriculum.
- Use of tablets and other touch screen technology should be a priority from early years' settings onwards in order that the pupil accesses the same opportunities as his/her peers. Most mainstream/early years apps will be appropriate.
- All information presented on the interactive whiteboard should have as much kinaesthetic involvement as possible.
- Use programs to connect whiteboards to individual tablets to allow the pupil to have information directly and in front of them. Vice versa, the pupil's work can be displayed on the screen.
- The 'Clicker' program has grids that relate to topics, thereby allowing a pupil to produce work related to the class topic whilst reducing the writing demands and memory load.
- Word processors allow pupils to carry out a project that results in quantity and a pleasing appearance when completed.
- Use Internet images and inserted photographs to provide illustrations.
- Alternative equipment can be considered, e.g.

    - 'Big Keys' keyboard;
    - lower case options on a keyboard or through the use of stickers;
    - a range of mice, e.g. a roller ball, joystick or a smaller one for small hands.

- Touch screens are more easily accessible.

- A tablet computer also provides a light, easily accessed option.
- A number of changes can be made to the standard computer system to make it easier to use. Information can be found on the AbilityNet website that explains how to make changes to the mouse, keyboard and display options. This will be necessary to allow for slower processing speeds.
- Graphics and simple drawing programs overcome difficulties with fine motor skills.
- E-mailing and texting should still form part of taught communication.

Part V

Developing social inclusion for the pupil with Down's syndrome

25 Independence skills

In addition to their delayed motor skills, pupils with Down's syndrome have difficulty with self starting and problem solving within situations. It is therefore crucial that pupils are given the tools to achieve independence across all areas of school life from the very first day. They need to develop routines and strategies that avoid dependence on adult intervention and prompting. Pupils are motivated by watching peers achieve tasks and copying the same activity. Pupils find transferral of skills difficult and may require succinct practice of each individual skill separately.

Feeding

Pupils with Down's syndrome often exhibit difficulties with eating and diet in a variety of ways:

- intolerance of, or resistance to new food;
- overfilling the mouth and not chewing food sufficiently before attempting to swallow,
- requiring routines for meal times;
- an inability to problem solve, e.g. following a new routine in the dining hall;
- difficulty expressing likes and dislikes or requesting a favourite food;
- manipulating cutlery, opening containers.

Develop skills in the following ways

- Practise spooning sand, shaving foam.
- Slice soft food such as bananas before moving onto foods that give more resistance, e.g. apples.
- Carry out two-handed activities, e.g. peeling a banana, pouring from a jug whilst holding a cup.
- Roll playdough or plasticine and cut into sausage shapes with a knife and fork.

Developing strategies to improve feeding

- Teach how to eat appropriately, i.e. how to put the correct amount of food in the mouth, stop, then chew.
- Use a good peer role model for lunchtime.
- Have routines but try to have a little flexibility.
- Offer pictures of food and/or written prompts to aid selection.

- Packed lunches may be easier to eat and allow the pupil to have foods they enjoy but if a cooked lunch is preferred parents should have access to the weekly menu in order to rehearse choice making.
- Use appropriate cutlery, e.g. short moulded handles (IKEA cutlery), specialist adapted cutlery.
- Use non-slip matting such as a damp tea towel to stabilise bowls or plates.
- A noisy environment may be upsetting and a smaller quieter environment may be more suitable.
- Support the pupil to pace their eating; use a placemat with a visual reminder to chew properly.

Toileting

Pupils with Down's syndrome should begin toilet training once in school if they have not already done so. However, achieving continence may take longer and be more problematic than with other pupils. Due to difficulties with speech and language and with physical processing delays, children with Down's syndrome are very unlikely to ask to go the toilet until very late on in their continence development... unless it is to avoid another task!

Developing skills

- Where possible visit the toilet as a peer group activity in order that the pupil has the opportunity for peer modelling.
- Have specific times for the routine; a toilet symbol could be included in the daily timetable.
- Develop a complete routine for the whole toilet visit including all the small steps of undressing, sitting on the toilet, wiping, washing and drying hands.
- Make a visual timetable to match the routine (this could be a concertina type that is easily carried around) and use appropriate signing.
- The pupil needs to feel that they are wet when they have an accident, so they need to wear pants or pants inside of pull-ups.
- Use the toilet rather than a potty.
- Ensure the toilet is the correct size; a toilet reducer and footblocks may be necessary for a smaller pupil.
- Carry out the whole routine even if the toilet is not used.
- Use a reward chart for success on the toilet (it may be necessary to reward just sitting on the toilet, before moving to the next stage).
- Ensure consistency between home and school with the routines to be followed, the language used, the techniques used, e.g. does the boy sit or stand to use the toilet?
- Encourage parents to dress their children in clothes that are easy to re-adjust, e.g. loose clothing that is easy to pull up and down.

Be patient; it may be a slow process.

Dressing

Pupils with Down's syndrome may have a delay or difficulty with dressing skills for a number of reasons:

- lack of motivation;
- poor problem solving skills;
- restricted gross and fine motor skills.

The following suggestions may help:

- Develop movements for putting on clothes, e.g. quoits over wrists, ankles and hoops up to the waist and over the head, before practising dressing skills.
- Play games to practise skills, e.g. dressing up with large clothes in the house corner.
- Backward chaining would be a useful method to teach the putting on of items of clothing, e.g. putting on trousers:
  - help the pupil put trousers on up to knees; the pupil pulls the trousers up independently;
  - help the pupil put trousers on up to ankles; the pupil pulls trousers up independently;
  - help the pupil put one leg in; the pupil continues;
  - the pupil is shown how to lay trousers out and put them on;
  - the pupil sits and puts trousers on independently.
- Practise doing fasteners on dolls that have large buttons, zips and Velcro® fastenings. Do laces on wooden shoeboxes or tie up parcels.
- Encourage independence skills from the earliest possible time, even if this is only for removing or putting on one item, e.g. a hat initially.
- Younger pupils may benefit from having all their belongings, bags, hats in a particular colour or with a certain logo, in order for them to be found more easily in the cloakroom.
- Encourage parents to dress their child in shoes with Velcro® fastenings, trousers/ skirts with an elasticated waist, school ties on elastic, clothes that are not tight (it may be necessary for uniform to have modifications to accommodate this).
- Promote independence by providing visual cue cards or lists to show what order clothes are taken off/put on, e.g. see figure.

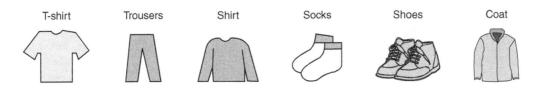

| T-shirt | Trousers | Shirt | Socks | Shoes | Coat |

- Provide trays or baskets to put clothes in when changing for PE to allow independent dressing.
- Encourage sitting to dress/undress, sitting with the back to a solid surface or holding onto a chair back to aid balance.
- Use T-shirts/sweatshirts with a logo/design on the front to help orientation of clothes.
- Give praise for effort when the pupil is trying to dress independently.
- Teach the pupil how to ask for assistance.
- Only help the pupil when he/she has tried for him/herself.
- Ensure the pupil does not miss out on playtime, etc. if he/she is slow to dress.

Older pupils

- Older pupils need to develop coping strategies to overcome their difficulties.
- Clothes need to be considered carefully to enable the pupil to have credibility with his/her peers.
- Consider how fashions can be adapted to make dressing easier.
- Adapt clothes with elastic, Velcro®, e.g. cut the school tie and join with Velcro®, adapt cuffs by putting in elastic to allow the hand to fit through.
- Some retailers supply school shirts with elasticated cuffs and top buttons; use 'curly laces'; wear polo shirts, jumpers with logos to help orientation, jumpers with raglan.

26 Developing self-esteem

The social strength of pupils with Down's syndrome means that they are very sensitive to how they fit into their world. Self-esteem can be easily dented if the child perceives that they are being treated differently or cannot achieve like everyone else.

There are a number of strategies that may help to build self-esteem.

- Praise everything! Every little task in life takes a huge amount of effort for the pupil with Down's syndrome to achieve. Reward with real congratulations. Body language is everything!
- Be specific in your praise. Say 'Great letter', not 'Good boy'.
- Make rewards appropriate to the pupil's level of development and straight after the event.
- Make all goals challenging but attainable.
- Set work at the appropriate level for the pupil's development.
- Convey by the adult's manner that the pupil is a valued member of the class.
- Have feedback sessions at the end of a lesson, which include an element of success.
- Display the pupil's work alongside other pupils' work.
- Acknowledge the pupil's strengths, e.g. politeness, kindness and perseverance.
- Raise the pupil's status within the group by giving jobs, e.g. being a monitor.
- Give all pupils the same opportunities.
- Ensure all staff are aware of the pupil's difficulties and support in the appropriate way.
- Ensure that staff share any successful strategies as the pupil moves through the school.
- Encourage the pupil to make contributions to his/her IEP and to be a part of the review process.
- Celebrate the pupil's success with their parents on the day it happens. The child may not be able to tell their parent why they got that sticker once they are at home or that they are going to be in assembly.

27 Supporting peers to include the pupil with Down's syndrome

In order to secure good social inclusion, typically developing children will also need support in developing appropriate behaviour towards the pupil with Down's syndrome. Peers need to be taught about their friend's needs in a sensitive way in order that they can develop a good understanding of how to relate effectively. Give clear explanations for expectations of behaviour alongside strategies that empower them to deal with their friend themselves. Often peers can develop behaviour that is too tolerant of their friend's difficulties. This inadvertently facilitates a continuation of the behaviour. Peers can also over compensate for their friends and this can lead to difficulties, where the pupil with Down's syndrome feels babied, rather than being treated as an equal.

Ways to foster inclusion

- Observations of the pupil with their peers will identify good interaction and any areas of difficulty. This is particularly important in unstructured situations.
- The following is a description of a situation that occurred with a six-year-old named Isaac but who in reality has a social age of a two-year-old. A group of pupils including Isaac, are taking part in outdoor play. Another pupil has told his teacher that Isaac has pushed him off the slide and he has hurt his leg. The teacher's first reaction is to tell Isaac off but ideally the situation should be considered using the 'Iceberg' theory in order to consider the wider picture:

  - Isaac is pushing;
  - Joe is crying;
  - When does it happen and why? Lack of social understanding. Lack of understanding. Lack of awareness of body space. Need for sensory feedback;
  - Is it a routine that is learnt at home or school?;
  - Isaac can't communicate that he wants to say 'weeeee' as a pupil goes down the slide.

- Strategies:

  1 Talk to parents about routines that may have developed.
  2 Identify – i.e. Isaac enjoys watching a child go down the slide and saying 'weeeee' as the child whizzes by so pushes the child to make it happen (Isaac is at the developmental stage of a two-year-old).
  3 Solutions:

     - Discuss issues with peers in circle time, friends group or in a Restorative Practice manner;

- Teach peers to say 'stop' using a hand/visual symbol;
- Develop social stories using photographs of appropriate play before play-time;
- Other children give stickers when Isaac engages in appropriate play with positive phrase, 'You were a good friend today Isaac'.

4 Distract behaviour by using a soft ball to whizz down the slide. Then move onto playing ball with another pupil.

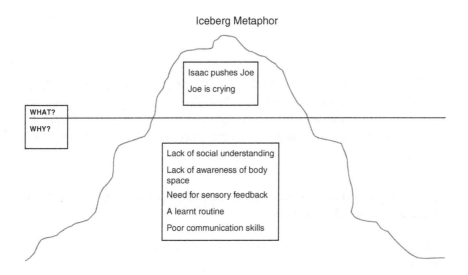

Iceberg Metaphor

Isaac pushes Joe
Joe is crying

WHAT?
WHY?

Lack of social understanding
Lack of awareness of body space
Need for sensory feedback
A learnt routine
Poor communication skills

28 Promoting peer-group relationships

Pupils with Down's syndrome are usually socially motivated and desperately want to be in the social mix, but may still have difficulty in managing and maintaining social relationships. In addition, other pupils in the peer group will need to be taught how best to include and respond to the pupil with Down's syndrome.

It may be necessary to consider ways to encourage good relationships between peers, through a variety of methods.

- Ensure the pupil is part of a signing school community that includes peers and staff, if this is their main form of communication.
- Pupils with Down's syndrome will watch and copy their peers, so therefore need strong, positive role models.
- In the Foundation Stage and Key Stage 1, develop other pupils' awareness of their peer with Down's syndrome characteristics, by sharing a personal book compiled by the parents or with their support, during circle time. Published books must be discussed first with parents and used publicly with great sensitivity.
- In Key Stage 2, set up a friendship group of pupils who would like to play with the pupil with Down's syndrome; weekly meetings could be held to discuss any positive features or difficulties. It may be necessary to support the group the pupil is choosing to play with.
- Be aware that speech and language difficulties can be a barrier to developing relationships and that it may be necessary to:

  - encourage play with other pupils with guidance of how to play;
  - develop understanding of the 'rules' of being a friend;
  - use role-play 'social stories', to teach more age-appropriate play and the unspoken rules of social interaction, including social scripts for involving self in play, e.g. 'Can I play?'

- Acknowledge that other pupils may be inclined to 'baby' the pupil with Down's syndrome, which should be discouraged. Teach the peer group how to encourage the pupil's independence instead.
- Peers should also be given verbal and non-verbal strategies to help them deal with any undesirable behaviour themselves. Peers could also use an agreed reward strategy themselves for praising good friend behaviour, e.g. giving a sticker.

- Adults should be sensitive to the pupil's need to have 'space' at break times. However, it may be necessary to pre-emptively intervene, e.g. to encourage making a choice at unstructured times, or to restart a play situation where loss of focus means trouble may be brewing.
- Organise structured play sessions led by a support assistant in the playground (if necessary), e.g. playing ring games, skipping games, ball games, imaginative play.
- Recognise that the pupil may need different approaches, e.g. to managing social relationships, but allow other pupils to recognise fair play.
- Pupils with Down's syndrome can benefit from working with more able pupils if their work is suitably differentiated.
- Encourage co-operative learning by working with a partner or in a small group. Again, a more mature peer is likely to be a useful workmate.
- Acknowledge the age of the pupil and allow him/her to be with his/her peers.
- Use peer support instead of adult support whenever possible.
- Encourage participation in lunchtime or after-school clubs.
- Encourage self-awareness, identity, self-esteem and self-confidence.

29 The pupils' views

The 2014 SEND Code of Practice states that:

Children have a right to be involved in making decisions and exercising choices. They have a right to receive and impart information, to express an opinion, and to have that opinion taken into account in any matters affecting them. Their views should be given due weight according to their age, maturity and capability.

(Articles 12 and 13 of the United Nations Convention on the Rights of the Child)

Pupils with Down's syndrome have very definite opinions about their lives and what they like and dislike. Communicating their wishes can be difficult but it is important that they have opportunities to do so. This will prevent them from *becoming passive* or exhibiting undesired behaviour because they are misunderstood or having others control them. The request could be their choice at lunchtime; alternatively, it could be as significant as making decisions about their future after leaving school. From the earliest days, pupils must be taught the skills that will allow them to exercise control over their lives.

Helping them make meaningful decisions about their life may be achieved in a variety of ways.

- In order for this to be possible an appropriate method of communication should be determined.
- Teach the language of choice making. Early examples might be home books 'I like…,' 'I don't like…' or 'I want…'. This will then need to be generalised into day-to-day settings.
- Use visual supports, e.g. pictures of food choices at lunchtime, rehearse the language for choice making using sentence prompts.
- Teach and practise request making in lots of different situations, through games, social communication groups etc.
- Give real experiences of the choices so that they can make a meaningful decision, e.g. visiting two alternative college placements.
- Use Social Stories across many aspects of life.

Careful thought should be given about how views are asked for. Language impairment results in significant difficulties in understanding the kinds of questions often used to solicit the pupil's view, e.g. for an Annual Review. However, pupils often know what the socially acceptable answer is and will give this rather than one that reflects their view.

An advocate could be used if a pupil or young person has difficulty speaking for themselves. They could help in the following ways:

- Helping the pupil or young person to be involved in and understand proceedings or decisions that are being made, think about their options and say what they want.
- Asking questions on their behalf.
- Making sure that the voice of the child or young person is heard and responded.
- To work to make things happen and change; by asking the right questions and finding out information help children and young people to make choices and have more control of their own life.

30 Home/school liaison

> Early years providers, schools and colleges should fully engage parents and/or young people with SEN when drawing up policies that affect them. Enabling parents to share their knowledge about their child and engage in positive discussion helps to give them confidence that their views and contributions are valued and will be acted upon.
>
> (2014 SEND Code of Practice)

There are a number of considerations that can be made in order to foster good home/school partnerships.

- Value the information that parents give about their child.
- Parents should be aware of the SEND Code of Practice and its implications for them.
- They should be invited to contribute to Learning Support Plans/IEP, attend review meetings and discuss how they can support the LSP/IEP.
- Provide reports for parents prior to Annual Reviews.
- Parents should know whom to contact if they have concerns about their child, for example:

  - class teacher;
  - SENCO;
  - headteacher;
  - special needs governor.

- Parental concerns should be listened to, acknowledged and addressed.
- Involve parents if the pupil is perceived to be having difficulties in school and seek co-operative solutions.
- Encourage parents to become involved in the life of the school, e.g. as reading partners, helpers on school trips or school governors.
- Inform parents of visits from other professionals, e.g. educational psychologist, speech and language therapist, and ensure any relevant reports are shared.
- Consult parents when changes in provision are being considered.
- Ensure parents are aware that their child's work is valued, e.g. through including his/her work in displays.

- Use a home/school diary to allow school and home to create a dialogue about the pupil's home and school life, which will overcome restricted language skills. This should preferably be written in the first person so the child is sharing the story of their day, e.g. 'I painted a picture'. The 'Special Stories' app is useful for this.
- Avoid discussions about their child within the hearing of other parents. Pupils should not be hearing negative comments about themselves.
- Give positive messages to the parent about their child; if problems arise find solutions in a productive manner. Be aware that parents do not want to fear the teacher coming to them at the end of the day!

31 The emotional aspects of life with a child with Down's syndrome

Families respond to the diagnosis of Down's syndrome in their own individual ways. Some families may be aware prior to birth but for some the knowledge comes as a shock after the birth of their child. In the months and years that follow, the families start the process of readjustment. Many of the emotions experienced will follow a pattern similar to that of bereavement and each family member may be at a different stage in the process of understanding and accepting the needs of their child.

- Initial feelings of grief are usually for the child that they thought they would have and now have lost.
- Acceptance of their child and coming to terms with his/her difficulties follows the realisation that children with Down's syndrome are first and foremost children but that they do need more help to overcome their problems.
- Grief may resurface at different milestones in their child's life, e.g. at secondary transition.
- Parents attend very many appointments with their children and this can be emotionally exhausting as each is a reminder of a layer of difficulty faced by them and their child.
- Parents often get very weary of being more expert than the experts and having to fight to access appropriate levels of care for their child.
- Managing the child's behaviour, including sleep disturbance, may be unlike that of previous children and parents may find it exhausting and may have difficulty coping.
- Accessing child care and/or baby sitters may be more difficult than for other parents.
- Extended family members may question the approaches suggested by professionals, intended to support the child and its family, thus undermining the parents, and leaving them feeling isolated.
- As the parents look to the long-term future there will be anxiety about what will become of their child.

32 Siblings of the pupil with Down's syndrome

Children who have a brother or sister with Down's syndrome may need special consideration in school.

- Changes in their behaviour may indicate they are experiencing emotional difficulties that are related to issues around their sibling with Down's syndrome, and they may require understanding and support.
- They may feel that things are not fair and more attention is given to their sibling with Down's syndrome.
- They may feel embarrassed about their brother's or sister's behaviour on some occasions.
- They may take undue responsibility for their sibling.
- They may worry about their brother or sister.
- They may feel unduly protective towards their brother/sister and demonstrate anger at pupils who try to tease or bully (any issues should be addressed at school).
- Some children may feel guilty about their feelings for their brother/sister.
- They may be teased or bullied because of a sibling with Down's syndrome (any issues should be addressed at school).
- They may need understanding from staff if their sibling with Down's syndrome causes them to be late, forget PE kit, have homework disturbed.

Part VI

Assessment and planning

33 Assessment

The assessment of pupils with Down's syndrome can pose difficulties due to a number of issues. Poor language skills can result in the pupil not understanding the task. This can then result in a lack of co-operation due to anxiety related to the situation. Restricted recording skills and a lack of ability to remain on task further exacerbates the situation.

However, formative assessment is required in order to inform and facilitate learning by identifying personalised learning goals and to develop appropriate activities to meet these goals. Furthermore, assessment in some format will be considered necessary to show progress to parents, governors and bodies such as Ofsted.

Schools must weigh up (in consultation with parents/carers) the value of formal assessments. If it is considered appropriate to assess a pupil, schools can make their own arrangements for pupils with Down's syndrome in internal exams.

However, for public or national exams like GCSEs, special arrangements can be requested. Schools have to show that pupils need special arrangements, through testing by a specialist teacher or an educational psychologist, to determine which arrangements would be appropriate.

The following special arrangements can be requested:

- extra time and/or rest breaks;
- one-to-one or small group working;
- a quiet area;
- exam papers in different formats, e.g. digital format;
- support teachers to act as an amanuensis or reader;
- alternative method of recording, e.g. this may be the use of a laptop.

Supporting the assessment process:

- give one-to-one work with a familiar support worker;
- use the normal method of communication to give instructions;
- provide concrete objects;
- use the normal method of recording, e.g. a laptop;
- provide a reader and a scribe.

The following documents may give some guidance:

- The 'DfE 2014 Key Stage 1 Assessment and Reporting Arrangements' state that any pupil below level 1 does not have to do the tests/tasks. A pupil above this but with SEN who cannot access the tests does not have to do them.
- Assessment and reporting arrangements Key Stage 2, www.gov.uk give some guidelines for Key Stage 2 SATs testing
- Teacher assessment should be used if standardised testing is not appropriate.

A range of assessment tools are available for tracking a SEN pupil's progress:

Bsquared (www.bsquared.co.uk) is a standardised assessment package to help schools assess small steps of progress. It covers all areas of the curriculum.

PIVATS (www.lancashire.gov.uk) is a system to inform target setting for pupils of all ages whose performance is outside national expectations and can be used to complement work alongside statutory key stage assessment.

CASPA (www.caspaonline.co.uk) is a tool for analysis and evaluation of attainment and progress for pupils with SEN.

34 Pupil profiles and learning plans/IEPs

> It is for schools and academies to determine their own approach to record keeping. But the provision made for pupils with SEN should be accurately recorded and kept up to date. Ofsted will expect to see evidence of the support that is in place for pupils and the impact of that support on their progress.
>
> (Special Educational Needs and Disability Code of Practice, 2014)

Appropriate expectations

Because the specific learning profile for Down's syndrome is uneven, with pupils experiencing significantly more difficulty in some areas than others, it would be expected that pupils will exhibit a range of abilities across the curriculum. It is still likely, however, that the Learning Plan/IEP would cover all areas across the curriculum since all are likely to show some degree of delay and will require differentiated strategies.

Setting targets

When writing Learning Plans/IEPs, it is crucial that targets are very tightly focused, cover very small steps and follow a SMART (Specific, Measurable, Achievable, Relevant, Timebound) type approach, rather than picking out the equivalent statement of attainment from the curriculum. This will be far too broad and unachievable. It is not even acceptable to have a statement from a P scale. The use of an assessment tool such as Bsquared is helpful in formulating sufficiently small steps.

The following are examples of methods of recording goals, activities and support that will help the pupil make progress. They are extracts and as such do not cover all the areas that would be necessary in a full Learning Plan/IEP. Plans must cover all relevant core curriculum areas as well as other deficit skills and sensory impairment areas. These will need to be informed by the relevant professional. These may be determined by individual schools, academies and local authorities. They should be reviewed termly and the responsibility of the parent, pupil and school should also be identified.

The following pen pictures describe pupils of different ages and are followed by examples of Learning Plans/IEPs that aim to address the key issues.

Leanne

Leanne is a 4-year-old who is in Foundation Stage. Her receptive language is much better than her expressive language; she is developing these skills by using signing. She can use approximately 30 signs for naming and requesting familiar objects. She enjoys adult-led activities rather than playing with her peers. Leanne is not yet hand dominant and uses an immature palmar grasp when making marks on paper. She can use a variety of apps on the iPad, which she finds very engaging. Leanne is not yet toilet trained and has bowel problems that complicate the development of this.

Fred

Fred is a happy, sociable 6-year-old boy who is a well included member of his class. He has a language delay, but uses simple sentences to communicate ideas and interact with his peers. He wears glasses. Fred has a limited concentration span and needs frequent changes of activity. He can be resistant to adult-directed activities and has been known to hide under the table. He has poor fine motor skills and uses an immature tripod grip to make attempts to write his name. He can count a number of objects but cannot record the numbers. He can read 30 key words and compose a simple phrase in response to a picture (with prompts) but cannot record the phrase without ICT support. He enjoys playing games on the computer. Fred has a previously repaired heart condition and is coeliac.

Poppy

Poppy is a very independent 9-year-old who likes to be in involved in all aspects of life. She has some language delay but is very intelligible when speaking to others. She has a good understanding of boundaries and is mostly compliant of them but does like to be in control and can sometimes resort to physical tactics with peers if she doesn't get her own way. She has good reading skills and a broad spelling vocabulary, but working memory difficulties limit her ability to write independently. She has both hearing and visual impairments including nystagmus.

Mary

Mary is a petite, shy 12-year-old who has very good language skills and is able to communicate easily, particularly with people with whom she is familiar. She has medical problems (a heart problem that has been resolved, stomach ulcers and rheumatoid arthritis), which cause frequent absences from school. The physical demands of a large secondary school, frequent class changes, the distances involved in movement around school, and carrying equipment, can be very tiring. Mary is also very strong-willed and is not averse to absenting herself from lessons. Mary has to work hard to maintain friendship groups because of frequent absences.

Inclusive school			
Name: Leanne	**Date of birth:** 04.01.11		
Strengths: Visual learning; signing; enjoys outdoor play; enjoys adult-led activities.			
Targets	**Strategies**	**Resources**	**Evaluation**
To understand and sign farm animal words in preparation for farm visit. Pig Sheep Cow	Learn signs for words. 'See and Learn' farm animals cards and iPad: matching words to words, then word to picture using sign and word simultaneously. Sing 'Old MacDonald'. Play with farm/puppet/toddler farm toys.	Display signs next to pictures in classroom. 'Special Words' app. iPad. Singing Hands 'Old MacDonald'.	
Cow Horse Duck Hen	Read farm books and anticipate response using sign.		
To know and order the letters for own name.	• Recognise the letters using Jolly Phonics visual prompt. • Order magnetic letters onto a photocopied baseboard ensuring left to right movement. • Spell out name on Clicker Connect using grid only with letters of Leanne (ensure correct case). • Multi-sensory letter exploration: letter shapes in the air; write in sand, foam.	Jolly Phonics cards. Magnetic letters. Lentils, sand, shaving foam, finger paint. Clicker Connect/ iPad.	
To develop toilet routines.	• Signed visual timetable including toilet time; posting activities as each is completed. • Visiting the toilet when other children go. • Poster of steps to completing toilet task. • Choice activity when task is complete.	Visual timetable; post box Poster Choice board Spare pants! Toilet reducer Step	
Parental involvement: Leanne to start to wear pants in school. To use the same visual timetable at home to encourage toileting routines. Read farm books. Play 'I spy my name'. Post-it notes stuck round the house or labelling Leanne's things.			

Learning Plan EHCP			
Name: Fred			
Nature of pupil's strengths: Visual learning; reading; social skills; independence; ICT.			
Targets	**Strategies**	**Resources**	**Evaluation**
To articulate f correctly.	• Model correct position of teeth using mirror. • Fishing game with f words to catch. • F lotto. • I spy f book and game. • 'Articulation Station' app. • 'Pirate phonics' app.	Mirror Fishing game Lotto I spy f book and game 'Articulation Station' app 'Pirate phonics' app	
To discriminate between 'f' and 'v'.	• Sort a bag of objects into correct initial sound. • Articulate correct sound to 'Jolly Phonics' prompt card. • I spy with my little eye choosing from set of 2 sounds: 2 objects of each sound (much harder).	f/v sound bag 'Jolly Phonics' cards f/v objects	
To read key words I /can/see/ the. To spell key words I /can/see/ the.	• Use word to word matching board or 'Special Words' app and iPad. • Making words with magnetic letters onto printed baseboard, moving to reducing visual support until ordering letters for each word independently. • Making letter shapes in the air. Multi-sensory approach. • Then use 'Big Keys' keyboard/Clicker app to type words from a model, removing visual support until typed to spoken response only.	Matching board; iPad and 'Special Words'. Magnetic letters. Sand, shaving foam, chalks, large felt tip pens, large paintbrushes and newspaper. Clicker program. 'Big Keys' keyboard. Flashcards. PM Starter books to match words being learnt.	

Targets	Strategies	Resources	Evaluation
To record a simple phrase in response to a picture/object (adult to prompt language). Fred to record with independence.	Order word cards to form sentence to picture prompt, using baseboard of sentence initially. Sentence starts: 'I can see ….' To type sentence using Clicker program.	Sentence in word cards from lotto above. Pictures/objects to match class room work. Clicker program with grid containing words 'I can see' plus appropriate topic words.	
To develop a more appropriate response to an adult request, i.e. moving to another activity.	Indicate expected activities using a visual timetable showing work plus reward. One-minute warning given of a change of activity. Talking tin button pressed by Fred to mark end of activity.	Visual timetable composed of photographs of work plus reward of computer time. Post box. Talking tin with 'finished' recorded on it.	
Parental involvement: Weekly spellings: I /can/ see/ the practised at home using same magnetic letter or computer strategy as school. To give photographs, objects of weekend activities to prompt language for discussion and recording. He will also require an Individual Health Care Plan.			

Academy			
Name: Poppy	**Date of birth:** 14.03.05		
Strengths: Poppy is independent and sociable; has good intelligibility; has good reading and handwriting skills.			
Targets	**Strategies**	**Resources**	**Evaluation**
To be able to independently record a sentence of up to 6 words created from personal/familiar experiences.	Record sentence onto iPad/Dictaphone. TA to write sentence on cards to rehearse using the sequential card concealing strategy. Poppy then to record sentence using laptop.	Home/school diary with comments/ pictures about activities that have taken place at home/school.	
To develop social skills to enable interaction and participation with peers at break without dominating.	Provide choice of apparatus for games. Provide a friendship circle where each can take turns to choose a game from an agreed set of structured games, shown on a choice board. Teach peers and Poppy appropriate scripts for when situation is both un/ successful.	Balls, ropes, hoops, skittles, props for imaginative games. Choice board. Written social scripts.	
To recognise coins to £1. To make 5p using 2p and 1p combinations.	Match/select/name coin lotto board and bingo using REAL coins and purses. Stick coins onto Numicon and make up 5 using 1s overlaying onto the 5 piece, moving to a mixture of 1s and 2s; then match out the equivalent coins. Use coins to 'buy' equivalent 2p and 1p sweets with an adult, then with peers.	Real coins. Purses. Cash till, shopping items. Numicon.	
Parental involvement: Contributions to home/school diary. Shopping with parents, giving opportunities to buy with 1p and 2p.			

Name: Mary	Date of birth: 19.05.01		
Strengths: Visual learner; articulate.			
Targets	**Strategies**	**Resources**	**Evaluation**
To maintain friendships during absence.	Use of IT. Circle of friends who are encouraged to keep in touch with Mary. On-going 'buddy' system organised by older pupils. Parent to be kept informed of school activities via e-mail.	Mobile phone, access to Internet, e-mail, messaging.	
To attend lessons.	Timetable with class number and photo. TA to rehearse next lesson content. Buddy of choice per lesson with iPod. Incentive to arrive at lessons; early arrival results in time to listen to One Direction on iPod until teacher's arrival. Handover box for iPad ready for work and iPod for transferral to next lesson. Photograph good work on iPad to show others.	A variety of sizes of timetables available. iPod. iPad with app link to interactive whiteboard.	
To reduce fatigue.	Use of a locker/drop off point to reduce amount of equipment carried. Registration room on ground floor. Minimum amount of equipment to be carried around. Spare set of books to be kept in the subject rooms. Access to drink/snack. Reduce lesson length/high level content to take account of Mary's tolerance levels. Provide downtime to catch up/ do home work/low demand task with high reward.	Key attached to trouser pocket for locker. Spare set of books for each subject. Water, dried fruit available. TA available. Access to quiet space.	
Parental involvement: Parents to provide mobile phone, encouragement to keep in touch with friends. Parents to support timetabling and equipment organisation.			

35 Transition to adulthood

> Pupils should be supported.... in decisions about their transition to adult life. They should also be involved in discussions about the schools and colleges they would like to attend. EHC plans should reflect this important ambition.
>
> (2014 SEND Code of Practice)

Local authorities, education providers and their partners should work together to help children and young people achieve successful long-term outcomes, such as getting a job or going into higher education, being able to make choices about their support and where they live, and making friends and participating in society. Raising aspirations is crucial if young people are to achieve these goals.

- Planning needs to start early on, from Year 9 at the latest; pupils with an EHCP (and those without) should have a review during which planning for the future is discussed.

The following should be considered:

- current skills and interests;
- future education;
- employment;
- housing.

Remember also:

- Some pupils may lack the cognitive ability to make decisions about their future.
- The accessible method of communication for the pupil should be taken into consideration, e.g. pictures rather than too much speech and inappropriate language.
- Pupils may have difficulty considering the possibilities for their future and dealing with change.
- Role models with the same interests may provide ideas.
- Providing contextualised experiences may make possibilities more real, e.g. work experience, further education placements, types of accommodation.
- The Children and Families Bill gives significant rights directly to young people once they reach 16. When a young person is over 16, local authorities and other

agencies should normally engage directly with the young person, ensuring that as part of the planning process, they identify the relevant people who should be involved, and how to involve them.

For those moving to further education the 2014 SEND Code of Practice suggests:

- the involvement of staff from the college's learning support team in the school-based transition reviews;
- an orientation period during the summer holidays, to enable the student to find his/her way around the college campus and meet the learning support staff;
- opportunities to practise travelling to and from college;
- the development of an individual learning programme outlining longer term goals covering all aspects of learning and development, with shorter term targets to meet the goals;
- supported access to taster sessions over a first year in college;
- a more detailed assessment of the young person's needs and wishes provided by learning support tutors during a taster year;
- staff development to ensure an understanding of the student's particular method of communication;
- use of expertise in accessing technology to identify appropriate switches, communication boards to facilitate the student's involvement in an entry level course;
- appropriate use of ICT to enable access to the curriculum;
- courses normally covered in one year planned over two years to meet the young person's learning needs;
- the young person should have dedicated access to ICT as their mode of learning.

When a young person with an education health and care (EHC) plan takes up a place in higher education, their EHC plan will cease. Local authorities should plan a smooth transition to the Higher Education Institution concerned (and, where applicable, to the new local authority area) before ceasing to maintain the young person's plan. Once the young person's place has been confirmed at the Higher Education Institution, the local authority **must** (with the young person's permission) pass a copy of their EHC plan to the relevant receiving establishment.

(2014 SEND Code of Practice)

Part VII

Continuing Professional Development

36 Planning for continuing professional development (CPD)

The majority of pupils with Down's syndrome are in mainstream schools. It is therefore important that all staff (including teaching assistants, lunchtime supervisors and support staff) feel able to meet their needs. The provision of carefully tailored CPD will help to build colleagues' confidence in this area and develop a consistent approach through the school.

An outline plan of CPD sessions might incorporate objectives such as ensuring that colleagues have:

- a profile of a pupil with Down's syndrome;
- a sound knowledge of the issues involved in teaching pupils with Down's syndrome;
- a range of strategies to meet individual needs and reduce barriers to learning;
- the confidence to ask experienced colleagues for help and advice.

It is advised that schools seek this training from a Down's syndrome specialist advisory teacher.

Following up initial training

Follow-up work to consolidate and build on the training delivered can be planned. This provides good accountability evidence for senior managers and Ofsted, and demonstrates the school's (and SENCO's) effectiveness. Ideas for follow-up activities are suggested below.

- A regular 'surgery' where teachers and TAs can seek advice from the SENCO or an appropriate specialist teacher.
- Optional 'advanced' CPD for interested staff.
- Opportunities for teachers to observe intervention programmes – in your own school or elsewhere.
- A working party to trial a new approach or piece of new technology.
- An action-research project to test an intervention and report back to staff on its effectiveness.
- Classroom observations by the SENCO to monitor colleagues' effectiveness in providing for the needs of the pupil with Down's syndrome.
- Detailed tracking of children with Down's syndrome to monitor progress and evaluate strategies being used to support them.

Part VIII

Resources and useful contacts

37 Resources to support pupils with Down's syndrome

Resources to develop language		
Category	**Item**	**Supplier**
Oromotor exercises	Talktools	
Articulation/ Phonic scheme	Jolly Phonics Phoneme cards	Jolly Phonics Ltd www.jollylearning.co.uk
	Read Write Inc. Speed Sound Cards Sets 1-3	Oxford University Press Amazon
	See and Learn: Speech (Playing with Sounds; Putting Sounds Together; Saying Words/More Words/Later Words)	Down Syndrome Education International www.seeandlearn.org
Reading	See and Learn Language and Reading programme	Down Syndrome Education International
	See and Learn: First Word Pictures	www.seeandlearn.org
	See and Learn: First Written Words	www.specialiapps.co.uk
	See and Learn: First Sentences	Appstore/Google Play/ Windows Store/ Amazon
	Full scheme available as See and Learn: Language and Reading First Steps Set	
	Also available in app form for iPad/ Android/ Windows 8.1/ Kindle Fire as: Special Words	

© 2016, *Supporting Children with Down's Syndrome,* L. Bentley, R. Dance, E. Morling, S. Miller and S. Wong, Routledge

Category	Item	Supplier
	POPS reading scheme	Down Syndrome Education International www.dseenterprises.org
	Oxford Reading Scheme for iPad	Appstore
	PM Starters reading books	Nelson Thornes
	Reading Helper	Reading Helper Tel: 0113 257 7796
	Reading Window/Ruler	LDA, TTS
	Coloured Overlays	TTS
Language	A Reading and Language Intervention for Children with Down Syndrome	Down Syndrome Education International www.dseenterprises.org
	Language for Thinking: S. Parsons and A. Branagan	Speechmark www.speechmark.net
	Pictoys: for practising auditory memory	CLEAR resources www.clear-resources.co.uk
	Special Stories app for Apple and Android	www.specialiapps.org
	Touch Words app – first 28 pictures and words from See and Learn programme for Apple and Android Also Touch apps for Colours/Numbers/Shapes/Animals/Emotions	www.specialiapps.org
	Sentence Builder app Part of a set of SALT apps	Mobile Education Store
	Sentence Maker app One of lots of good apps by this maker	Innovative Investments Limited
	See and Learn Language and Reading (see Reading section above)	Down Syndrome Education International www.seeandlearn.org
Language/ behaviour support	Talking Tins	Widely available on the internet, try www.primaryclassroom resources.co.uk/teaching

© 2016, *Supporting Children with Down's Syndrome,* L. Bentley, R. Dance, E. Morling, S. Miller and S. Wong, Routledge

Category	Item	Supplier
Maths	Numicon	Oxford University Press Amazon Down Syndrome Education Enterprises
	Special Numbers app for Apple devices	www.specialiapps.org Appstore
	See and Learn Numbers	www.seeandlearn.org
Memory	See and Learn Memory	www.seeandlearn.org
	Match and Find app	www.specialiapps.co.uk

Resources to support fine motor development		
Category	Item	Supplier
Fine motor skills box	Skill development	tts-group.co.uk
Scissors	Mounted table top scissors	Peta (UK) Ltd and tts-group.co.uk
	Pushdown table scissors	As above
	Dual control training scissors (L & R)	As above
	Mini easy grip (loop) scissors	As above
	Long loop scissors (L & R)	As above
	Self opening scissors	As above
	Self opening long loop scissors	As above
	Comprehensive assessment kit	As above
	Fiskar squeezers	NES Arnold
	Fiskar junior scissors (L & R)	As above
	Fiskars for kids	As above
	Self-opening scissors (L & R)	Smith and Nephew, Homecraft
Developing cutting skills	Programme to support cutting skills	LDA
	Developing scissor skills	Peta (UK) Ltd
Pencil grips	Tri-go	Taskmaster Ltd
	Stubbi (same as Stetro)	As above

© 2016, *Supporting Children with Down's Syndrome,* L. Bentley, R. Dance, E. Morling, S. Miller and S. Wong, Routledge

Category	Item	Supplier
	Ultra grip	As above
	Comfort grip	As above
	Crossguard	As above
	Claw grip	As above
	Handi writer (puts pencil into web of hand)	TTS
Dycem	Non-slip material on roll	Patterson medical
	Self-adhesive strips (to make non-slip rulers)	As above
Sloping writing surface	Write Angle	Completecareshop 0845 5194 734
	Writestart Desk	LDA
	Posture Pack	Back in Action Tel: 020 7930 8309
Pencils	Writestart pencils	Variety of sources on line
	Berol Handhugger pencils	As above
	Noris Triplus Triangular pencils	As above
	S move pens and pencils (left handed and right handed)	www.stabilo.com or many stationers
Pens	Berol Handhugger fibre tip pen	As above
	Rubber barrel pens with varying flow/resistance	Most stationery shops
Handwriting programmes	Write from the Start Book 1 and 2 by Teodorescu and L. Addy	Available from Internet sources
Compass Rulers	Safe drawing compass	Hope Education
	Alligator easi grip ruler	NES Arnold, Taskmaster
	Make your own non-slip ruler using 2 × 1 cm strips of self-adhesive Dycem to the back of the ruler	
Construction toys	Stickle bricks	Yorkshire Purchasing Organisation
	Magnetic blocks Clic	

© 2016, *Supporting Children with Down's Syndrome*, L. Bentley, R. Dance, E. Morling, S. Miller and S. Wong, Routledge

Resources to support PE		
Beanbags	Available as rabbits, frogs and turtles	NES Arnold
	Sensory ball pack	Yorkshire Purchasing
Balls	Spordas spider ball	NES Arnold
	Koosh ball	As above
	Tail ball	As above
	Floater ball (large, light, slow-moving)	As above
	Plus balls (inflatable paper balls – very slow)	As above
	Easy Katch ball (tendrils)	Hope Education
	Rubber flex Graballs	As above
	Bump ball (easy catch)	tts-group
	Sure grip netball	tts-group
	Play catch net	Cost Cutters educational suppliers
Group work equipment	Balance sets	Hope Education
	Agility ladder	TTS
	Tactile discs (stepping game)	TTS
Basketball	Adjustable height basketball net	As above
	Little Sure Shot	Hope Education

Resources to support food technology		
Non-slip mats	Dycem mats available individually or on a roll	ROMPA 08452301177
Holding equipment	Clyde grater, scraper and spike – to hold vegetables, and integral grater on a non-slip base	Complete careshop 0845 194 734
	Food preparation system – for use by those who have difficulties gripping	As above
	Pan handle holder – to prevent the pan moving while stirring with one hand	As above
	Kettle tilt – to assist with pouring	As above
Alternative cutting equipment	Rapid chopper – a single hand operated chopper with an integral blade	As above

© 2016, Supporting Children with Down's Syndrome, L. Bentley, R. Dance, E. Morling, S. Miller and S. Wong, Routledge

Resources to support recording skills		
Spelling	An Eye for Spelling by Charles Cripps	LDA
	Starspell (computer program)	Inclusive Technology
	Toe by Toe by Keda and Harry Cowling	Toe by Toe (ISBN 0952256401)
Number Recording	Numbershark (computer program)	Inclusive Technology
	Co:Writer (word prediction)	Don Johnston
	Clicker software Clicker apps	Crick Software Ltd www.cricksoft.com
	WriteOnline App	Crick Software
	Special Stories	Special

ICT equipment		
Keyboard letter stickers	Lower case stickers for younger pupils	Inclusive Technology
Big Keys	Large keys (upper or lower case)	Inclusive Technology, SEMERC
Alternative mice	Roller balls etc.	Inclusive Technology
Keyboard letter stickers	Lower case stickers for younger pupils	Inclusive Technology

Publications		
Teachers Standards, 2012	Department for Education	www.education.gov.uk/schools
2014 SEND Code of Practice	Department for Education	www.gov.uk
Supporting pupils with a medical need in schools, 2014	Department for Education	www.gov.uk
Pivats		www.lancashire.gov.uk
BSquared		www.bsquared.co.uk
CASPA		www.caspaonline.co.uk
Writing Handwriting	IPaSS	01482 318400
Ready Steady…go to PE	IPaSS	01482 318400

© 2016, *Supporting Children with Down's Syndrome,* L. Bentley, R. Dance, E. Morling, S. Miller and S. Wong, Routledge

38　Useful contacts

Down Syndrome Education International
www.dseinternational.org
6 Underley Business Centre
Kirkby Lonsdale
Cumbria
LA6 2DY
UK
0300 330 0750
info@dseinternational.org

Down's Syndrome Association
www.downs-syndrome.org.uk
Langdon Down Centre
2a Langdon Park
Teddington
Middlesex
TW11 9PS
info@downs-syndrome.org.uk

Special Olympics
18 Grosvenor Gardens
London SW1 0DH
Tel: 020 7824 7800

Appendix 1

Issues for consideration

Issues to be considered by the governors and senior management when including a pupil with Down's syndrome:

Issue	✓	✗	Action
Is the governing body aware of the pupils with special educational needs and its responsibilities in ensuring that the needs of these pupils are being met?			
Are the buildings and furniture accessible to all pupils?			
Is there any additional adult support for the pupil with Down's syndrome?			
Are all staff given time to train and update skills to meet the particular needs of the pupil with Down's syndrome, e.g. signing, ICT?			
Are there methods of ensuring effective communication between home and school?			
Are other agencies involved in meeting the needs of the pupil and is time given to meet with outside agencies?			
Is time given to discuss the changing needs of the pupil?			
Are staff aware of recent legislation, LA/SEND policies?			
Are strategies in place to support a pupil's emotional well-being?			
Is the governing body aware of the legislation relating to pupils with a medical need in school?			

© 2016, *Supporting Children with Down's Syndrome*, L. Bentley, R. Dance, E. Morling, S. Miller and S. Wong, Routledge

Issue	✓	✗	Action
Does the school have any necessary medical information for the pupil, e.g. heart problems, glue ear?			
Does the school promote positive images of the pupil and positive peer group relationships?			
Are appropriate teaching strategies in place?			
Are any additional resources/strategies required to support curriculum delivery and do staff know where to access these, e.g. step boxes to facilitate access, pencil grips, computer programs?			

© 2016, Supporting Children with Down's Syndrome, L. Bentley, R. Dance, E. Morling, S. Miller and S. Wong, Routledge

Appendix 2

Some professionals who may be involved
with the pupil

Professional	Personnel and contact number
Educational Psychologist	
Advisory teacher for Down's syndrome	
Educational Service for Physical Disability	
Speech and language therapist	
Visual Impairment Service	
Hearing Impairment Service	
School nurse	
Physiotherapist	
Occupational therapist	
Community paediatric nurse for Down's syndrome	

© 2016, *Supporting Children with Down's Syndrome*, L. Bentley, R. Dance, E. Morling, S. Miller and S. Wong, Routledge

Appendix 3
Small steps approach to recording progress in reading

	Started	Achieved	Comments
Shows interest in books			
Turns several pages at once			
Turns one page at a time			
Points to a named picture			
Turns pages to find a named picture			
Finds a named book on request			
Will sit and share book with an adult for an increasing amount of time			
Will sit in a small group to share a book			
Indicates what comes next in a repetitive story			

© 2016, *Supporting Children with Down's Syndrome,* L. Bentley, R. Dance, E. Morling, S. Miller and S. Wong, Routledge

	Started	Achieved	Comments
Matches objects to pictures			
Matches pictures to pictures			
Participates in a group lotto game			
Finds a name card when identified by a picture and name			
Matches name card to a corresponding name card from a selection of two			
Matches letters on a board game			
Matches words on a board game			
Finds a word amongst an increasing number of words			
Reads flash card words			
Reads words in books			

Name: ....

© 2016, *Supporting Children with Down's Syndrome,* L. Bentley, R. Dance, E. Morling, S. Miller and S. Wong, Routledge

Appendix 4
Small steps approach to recording progress in scissor skills

	Started	Achieved	Comments
Can crumple tissue paper			
Can tear tissue paper			
Can open and close scissors*			
Can snip with scissors with an adult to guide the movement			
Can snip without adult support			
Can snip to make a fringe			
Can cut a piece of card in two with an adult holding the card			
Can cut across a piece of card without help			
Can cut between two lines (reduce gap)			
Can cut along a broad felt tip line			

© 2016, *Supporting Children with Down's Syndrome,* L. Bentley, R. Dance, E. Morling, S. Miller and S. Wong, Routledge

	Started	Achieved	Comments
Can cut along a fine line			
Can cut between two lines that gently wave, build up the curves			
Can cut round a circle with concentric guidelines			
Can cut round a circle that has a broad felt tip outline			
Can cut round a square with broad parallel lines			
Can cut round a square with a thin outline			
Can cut out a variety of shapes			
*Can use trainer scissors or normal scissors. Card is easier to use than paper.			

Name: ....

© 2016, *Supporting Children with Down's Syndrome,* L. Bentley, R. Dance, E. Morling, S. Miller and S. Wong, Routledge